THE LYLE ANTIQUES & THEIR VALUES

KITCHENWARE

S0-FMH-491

THE LYLE ANTIQUES & THEIR VALUES

KITCHENWARE

Compiled by Anthony Curtis

While every care has been taken in the compiling of information contained in this volume the publishers cannot accept any liability for loss, financial or otherwise, incurred by reliance placed on the information herein.

All prices quoted in this book are obtained from a variety of auctions in various countries and are converted to dollars at the rate of exchange prevalent at the time of sale.

The words "Lyle Publications" and the "Silhouette" design are registered trademarks belonging to Coward-McCann, Inc.

Copyright © 1983 by Voorhoede Publicaties B.V.
No part of this book (issue) may be reproduced in any form by print, photoprint, microfilm or any other means without written permission from the publisher unless for review purposes.

Library of Congress Cataloging in Publication Data

Curtis, Tony
  Kitchenware.

  (The Lyle antiques and their values)
  Previously published as: Kitchen equipment.   1977.
  Includes index.
    1. Kitchen utensils—Collectors and collecting.
  2. Kitchen utensils—Catalogs.   I. Title.   II. Series.
  TX656.C87   1983   683'.8   83-720
  ISBN 0-698-11237-7 (Coward-McCann)

Printed in the United States of America
Distributed in the United States by Coward-McCann, Inc.,
200 Madison Avenue, New York, N.Y. 10016

INTRODUCTION

This book is one of a series specially devised to aid the busy professional dealer in his everyday trading. It will also prove to be of great value to all collectors and those with goods to sell, for it is crammed with illustrations, brief descriptions and valuations of hundreds of antiques.

Every effort has been made to ensure that each specialised volume contains the widest possible variety of goods in its particular category though the greatest emphasis is placed on the middle bracket of trade goods rather than on those once-in-a-lifetime museum pieces whose values are of academic rather than practical interest to the vast majority of dealers and collectors.

This policy has been followed as a direct consequence of requests from dealers who sensibly realise that, no matter how comprehensive their knowledge, there is always a need for reliable, up-to-date reference works for identification and valuation purposes.

When using your Antiques and their Values Book to assess the worth of goods, please bear in mind that it would be impossible to place upon any item a precise value which would hold good under all circumstances. No antique has an exactly calculable value; its price is always the result of a compromise reached between buyer and seller, and questions of condition, local demand and the business acumen of the parties involved in a sale are all factors which affect the assessment of an object's 'worth' in terms of hard cash.

In the final analysis, however, such factors cancel out when large numbers of sales are taken into account by an experienced valuer, and it is possible to arrive at a surprisingly accurate assessment of current values of antiques; an assessment which may be taken confidently to be a fair indication of the worth of an object and which provides a reliable basis for negotiation.

Throughout this book, objects are grouped under category headings and, to expedite reference, they progress in price order within their own categories. Where the description states 'one of a pair' the value given is that for the pair sold as such.

CONTENTS

KITCHENWARE

APPLE CORERS

Early 19th century apple corer, with ivory handle. $65

Georgian apple corer with turned ivory handle. $115

George III silver shovel spoon by Cocks & Bettridge, Birmingham, 1800. $150

Silver and ivory corer, 1811. $170

George III apple corer, London, 1808, 5in. long. $250

Silver apple corer, maker TH, circa 1710, 13.8cm. long. $350

Silver apple corer, circa 1685, 12.4cm. long, no marks. $400

Silver peeler and corer by Samuel Pemberton, 1803. $475

George III traveling apple corer by Joseph Willmore, Birmingham, 1814, 4in. long. $545

Queen Anne apple corer, 5in. long overall, by Thomas Kedden, London, 1704, 12oz. $1,000

ASPARAGUS TONGS

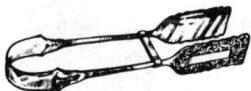

Asparagus tongs by Mappin and
Webb, Sheffield 1894. $180

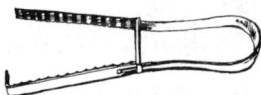

Early 19th century silver asparagus
tongs. $200

Silver asparagus tongs by J. Buckett
of London, circa 1770, 23cm. long.
                                              $225

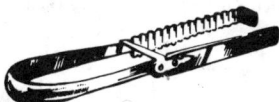

Pair of Georgian silver asparagus
servers. $245

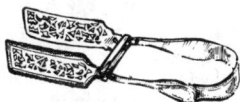

Silver asparagus tongs by G.W.
Adams, 1864. $250

Silver asparagus servers by
Thomas Northcote, 1790. $340

Silver asparagus tongs by William
Chawner, 10½in. long, 5.5oz., 1832.
                                              $350

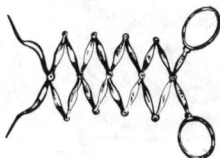

Pair of Scottish lazy tongs by
Hamilton & Inches, 1906, 48cm.
fully extended. $395

BARRELS

Victorian lead glazed
spirit barrel. $65

Biscuit colored stoneware
spirit barrel with brass tap,
circa 1860, 13¼in. high.
$80

Stoneware spirit barrel, with
a brass tap, circa 1840.
$90

One of a pair of spirit
barrels molded with
the Royal Arms and
Vines. $135

A steel banded oak cider
barrel with hand riveted
joints to bands, 11in.
diam. at top, circa 1840.
$145

Late 19th century
cut glass barrel
with a gun metal
tap. $145

Staffordshire white pottery
spirit barrel titled 'Brandy',
circa 1850, 12½in. high.
$215

A Victorian vinegar
barrel, in sand-
colored ironstone
with a raised Coat of
Arms. $235

One of a pair of Bristol
pearlware documentary
spirit barrels, 1834,
12cm. high. $975

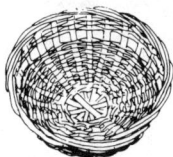

Victorian miniature
basket, about 4in.
across. $5

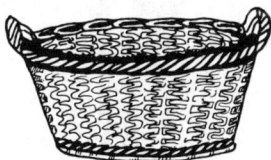

Victorian clothes basket. $10

A Regency waste
paper basket on
scroll feet $180

Royal Worcester basket in
the form of a bird's nest,
circa 1890, 6in. high.
$250

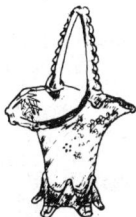

Late 19th century am-
berina basket, floral
decorated, 10½in.
high. $275

Hukin & Heath silver sugar
basket with incurved rim
and hinged handle, 6oz.,
London, 1881, 17cm. wide.
$360

George III boat-shaped
sweetmeat basket by
Peter and Ann Bateman,
London, 1799, 8oz.1dwt.,
6½in. wide. $665

Late 19th century/early
20th century enameled
silver mounted agate
sweetmeat dish, 15.5cm.
long. $870

Clear glass etched and enameled basket with gilded
metal handle, by Emile
Galle, 18cm. diam.
$2,260

11

KITCHENWARE

BEAKERS

Victorian cranberry glass beaker. $20

Victorian purple slag glass beaker. $35

Doulton stoneware beaker, showing golfers, circa 1900, 4¾in. high. $185

Unusual amber-flashed beaker of thistle form, circa 1850, 16.2cm. high. $315

Rosenberg 'eggshell' beaker and saucer, decorated by Sam Schellink, 1904. $320

Cylindrical silver beaker by A.B. & F.G., Moscow, 1792, 8.4cm. high. $450

Early George II flared cylindrical beaker by William Darker, London, 1727, 3oz., 3¼in. high. $725

Venice two-handled beaker vase on spreading foot, circa 1770 10cm. high. $775

Vienna Du Paquier tall slender beaker, probably by Carl Wendelin Anreiter von Zirnfeld, circa 1725. $1,295

Mid 19th century vaseline glass bell with diagonally ribbed body, and clear handle, 27cm. high. $70

A small, pierced and chased silver table bell. $75

19th century muffin seller's hand-bell, 10in. high, in perfect condition.$110

19th century cast brass bracket with original hanging bell, 14in. high. $175

Oriental bronze table bell, on carved and pierced ironwood stand. $180

Dolphin plated brass bell, circa 1860. $270

George III table bell by Abraham Portal, London, 1764, 6oz.11dwt., 4¾in. high. $775

George IV table bell by William Eaton, London, 1821, 3in. high, 4oz. 7dwt. $830

George II silver table bell by Thomas Whipham, 5½oz. $2,015

13

BELLOWS

20th century oak bellows with embossed brass facing. $45

19th century elm bellows. $55

Fine pair of Georgian bellows. $65

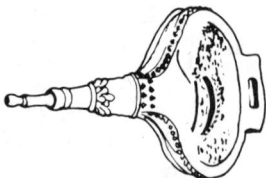

Walnut bellows, with carved landscape 'Auld Brig O' Doon'. $65

Victorian bellows with embossed brass facing depicting a domestic scene.
$75

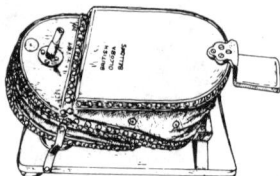

A large pair of foot operated bellows of elm and leather construction on baseboard, 1ft.9in. long, 1ft.2in. high.
$90

Elm bellows with brass center decoration piece, 25in. long, circa 1790.
$100

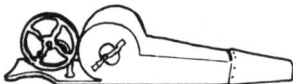

19th century oak and brass mounted fire blower. $100

Early 19th century carved oak bellows with brass finial. $100

Irish bellows in brass and mahogany. $125

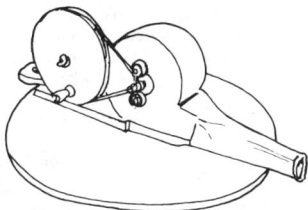

Late 19th century mechanical bellows in black painted cast iron and brass machine, 23½in. high. $170

18th century oak and brass bellows, 17in. wide. $240

Late 19th century mechanical bellows of black painted iron construction, 20in. high. $250

Early 19th century brass winding bellows. $430

One of a rare pair of Charles I bellows in elm and fruitwood, circa 1640, 2ft. long. $2,860

One of a pair of mid 16th century Italian oak bellows. $5,500

15

BISCUIT CONTAINERS

Victorian tin biscuit box decorated with a scene depicting two swans. $20

Huntley & Palmer pedestal biscuit tin decorated with classical figures. $35

Huntley & Palmer tin decorated with printed paper, circa 1900. $35

Oak biscuit barrel with EPNS fittings and a ceramic lining, circa 1910. $35

Edwardian C.W.S. biscuit tin. $40

An English tin container, in the form of a commode chest, circa 1890-1910. $45

Huntley & Palmer biscuit tin. $55

Huntley & Palmer laundry basket biscuit tin, circa 1904. $60

Jacob & Co., Coronation coach biscuit box, 1937. $90

BISCUIT CONTAINERS

Biscuit tin in the form of
a cannon. $90

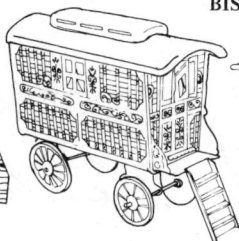

Jacob's gypsy caravan biscuit tin, circa 1905.
$100

Huntley & Palmer
library biscuit tin.
$100

WMF Art Nouveau wafer barrel
and lid. $150

**Library biscuit tin by
Huntley & Palmer, 1900.**
$115

Moorcroft Hazledene
biscuit jar and cover
painted in Moonlit
Blue pattern, 17cm.
high. $330

Biscuit tin in the shape of
a Mail van. $430

Electroplated beehive biscuit
box, by Martin, Hall & Co.
Ltd., circa 1875, 23.5cm.
high. $620

Cameo glass biscuit barrel,
electroplated mounts by W.
W. Harrison & Co., Sheffield,
circa 1885, 17cm. high.$830

17

BLUE & WHITE CHINA

Staffordshire soup bowl, circa 1825. $10

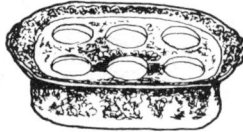

Spode, blue and white egg stand. $30

One of a pair of Ringtons square-shaped tea caddies transferred in blue, 10cm. high. $30

Blue and white transfer printed small oval dish, impressed Copeland, and number 6, circa 1850, 8½in. long. $45

One of a pair of late 19th century blue and white Delft style candlesticks. $55

Blue and white pictorial Spode ware ashet. $55

Small fan-shaped asparagus server in Caughley porcelain, circa 1780-90. $70

Caughley porcelain egg-drainer and 'waster', circa 1780-90. $90

A 19th century Worcester blue and white pickle dish. $145

Dublin delftware meat dish, Delamain's factory, circa 1760, 43cm. high. $250

Adams silver mounted blue and white mug with angular handle, London, 1802, 12.5cm. high. $365

Large Staffordshire platter with wide floral border, circa 1825, 19in. wide.
$375

Bristol delft blue and white plate with brick pattern rim, circa 1730, 21.5cm. diam. $385

Guangxu blue and white jar and cover with panels of flowers, 34cm. high, slightly chipped.
$605

Derby blue and white shell centerpeice by Wm. Duesbury & Co., circa 1770, 21.5cm. high. $820

One of a pair of Guangxu period blue and white jars and covers, 34cm. high. $845

Worcester blue and white chestnut basket, cover and ladle, circa 1770, 4½in. diam.$2,815

Rare Daoguang dated blue and white water jar and cover in bucket shape, 23.2cm. high. $14,400

19

BOTTLES

Small green tinted glass sauce bottle. $5

Brown glass beer bottle. $5

Elegant green glass beer bottle, circa 1890. $5

Sheared top sauce bottle of green tinted glass. $5

Bung stopper mineral water bottle. $10

Amber glass 'Hair Tonic' bottle. $10

One pint brown glass beer bottle. $10

Stoneware ginger beer bottle. $15

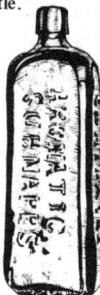

Victorian brown glass spirit bottle. $25

Victorian whisky
bottle. $15

'Dumpy' green glass
mineral water bottle.
$15

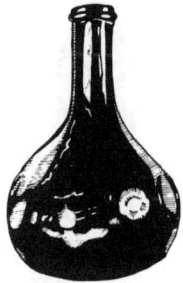

Green glass 'onion' bottle,
circa 1885. $20

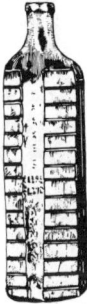

Clarke's clear fluid
ammonia bottle. $24

Dark green glass pickle
jar, 1880. $25

Codd's glass mineral
bottle with amber
stopper. $40

Red glass Barrel Bitters
bottle, American, circa
1860-80, 9¼in. high.$40

Glass wine bottle of
squat mallet shape,
neck with string rim,
20cm. high. $40

Amber glass Indian
Queen Bitters bottle,
circa 1870-80, 12¼in.
high. $50

21

BOTTLES

Codd's 'light bulb' bottle with black marble stopper. $50

Victorian embossed black glass whisky bottle. $60

Gigantic green glass bottle, mid 17th century, 15in. high. $90

Codd's amber glass mineral bottle. $110

Green blown glass bottle with etched decoration and dated 1829, 30cm. high. $125

Rare 'Bitters' bottle dated 1874. $160

Mid 19th century pressed amber glass Bitters bottle by A. M. Bininger & Co., 32cm. high. $180

American blown three-mold bottle in olive green glass, circa 1830, 17cm. high. $275

Sealed wine bottle, dark olive green, with kick-in base, circa 1765, 24cm. high. $340

H. Codd's cobalt blue
marble stoppered bottle.
$360

One of a pair of pressed
glass bar bottles with
flared bases, Sandwich,
Massachusetts, 10in.
high, circa 1850. $425

Rare early wine bottle, circa
1660, 8in. high. $430

French blown-in mold
Pocahontas bottle, circa
1830, 2 x 2¼in. $500

Blown-in mold bottle in
green color, New England,
circa 1825, 6¼in. high.
$900

Sealed and dated wine
bottle, inscribed I. Smith,
1706, 6¾in. high.
$1,690

Early sealed wine bottle,
circa 1683, 6in. high.
$1,845

17th century Dutch
sealed wine bottle,
shoulder applied with
armorial seal, 9½in.
high. $2,430

Rare and unrecorded early
sealed wine bottle, 7¼in.
high, circa 1670.
$4,275

23

BOWLS

Victorian earthenware mixing bowl. $10

A sugar bowl from the Dartmouth pottery, bearing the legend, 'Waste not, want not'. $10

'Quick-cooker' for making steak and kidney pudding, around 1890. $15

Mid 18th century Wedgwood basalt covered sugar bowl with two handles, 4¾in. diam. $50

An unusually large Welsh butter bowl of sycamore wood, circa 1790, 17in. diam. $100

A Sunderland ware bowl, with transfer printed panels, 12½in. diameter. $145

Early 19th century pinewood bowl, possibly American, 15in. diam. $145

Brass and copper bowl on lion paw feet, 18in. diam. $170

Amstel circular sugar bowl and cover with acorn finial, circa 1780, 11cm. high. $175

BOWLS

Ruskin eggshell pottery bowl, circa 1910. $180

Royal Doulton 'flambe' shallow circular bowl on pedestal foot, 18cm. diam. $275

Rare Lynn finger bowl of dark emerald green metal, circa 1765, 11.5cm. diam. $405

Rosenberg 'eggshell' bowl and cover, decorated by Roelof Sterken, 12cm. high, 1901. $410

Ansbach slop-bowl with trailing sprigs of leaves and flowers, circa 1770, 17cm. wide. $675

19th century Chinese Canton shallow bowl with flat rim, 13in. diam. $750

Liverpool bowl by William Ball, circa 1760. $1,520

Silvered copper ewer and bowl, ewer with riveted curved handle, circa 1904. $2,910

Capodimonte circular sugar bowl and cover, circa 1758, 10.5cm. diam. $8,165

BOXES

Miniature carved wood Scandinavian butter box, 4in. long. $85

Farmhouse salt box, circa 1780, 10¾in. high. $115

Coffee container, circa 1875. $135

George IV silver toothpick case, 2½in. wide, by Ledsham, Vale & Wheeler, Birmingham, 1827. $270

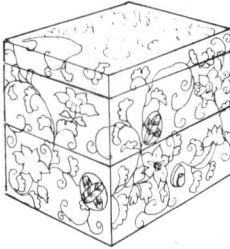

Two-tiered Japanese lacquer picnic box, 25in. wide. $450

19th century Scandinavian painted bride's box of plywood strips, 17½in. long. $450

Japanese lacquer picnic box of octagonal form with gilt decoration, 35cm. diam. $550

Chippendale octagonal mahogany bonnet box, circa 1760, 58cm. wide. $1,400

18th century American mahogany pipe box with wall attachment, 16½in. high. $1,400

BREAD BINS

Early 20th century enamel bread bin. $25

Victorian 'Improved Bread Pan' in earthenware.
$35

A heavily chased and embossed plated bread bin and cover. $155

BREAD HUTCHES

French 18th century walnut bread hutch, 32in. wide.
$1,645

Late 17th century yewwood bread cupboard.$2,170

Early oak food hutch.
$2,340

BREAD PEELS

Oven peel used in a brick oven. $75

A large wooden bread peel.
$90

Unusual oblong shaped wafer iron for making wafer bread. $110

BUCKETS

Antique leather fire bucket with coat of arms on front. $75

Large 19th century copper bucket with brass swing handle, 13in. diam. $120

Victorian fireman's leather bucket decorated with a coat of arms. $135

An attractive well bucket, with wrought iron swing handle and decorative riveted strength bands, circa 1790, 17in. high. $215

Dutch circular copper bucket with swing handle, 15in. diam. $260

Large Wemyss-ware slop bucket and cover, circa 1900, 29.4cm. high. $265

Dutch copper and brass peat bucket, circa 1770 16in. high. $325

A fine 18th century brass bucket. $630

Dutch tole-peinte tea bucket decorated with chinoiserie, circa 1800, 1ft.1in. wide. $805

George III brass bound bucket with swing handle. $835

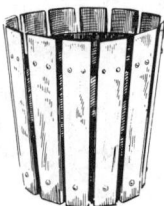

Gustav Stickley oak waste bucket, banded together with iron, 12in. diam. $950

George III mahogany circular bucket, bound in brass, 37cm. high. $1,040

Dutch floral marquetry oyster bucket with brass banding and handle, circa 1760, 13in. diam. $1,065

George III mahogany bucket with brass fittings, circa 1790. $1,170

Early 19th century Regency brass bound pail with brass liner and handle, 35.5cm. high. $1,400

George III mahogany boat-shaped oyster bucket with brass banding liner and handle, 14in. high, circa 1790. $1,470

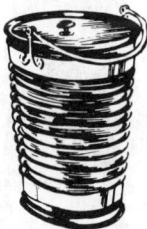

George III mahogany peat bucket with circular lid, circa 1765, 1ft.6in. high. $2,160

One of a pair of George III brass bound mahogany bottle carriers, 11¼in. high. $3,420

KITCHENWARE

BUTTER WORKERS

Pair of Victorian butter pats.
$10

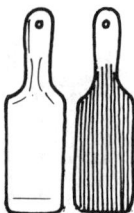

Butter pats for shaping.
$10

Butter worker used on a sloping tray. $20

BUTTER CHURNS

Table type box churn, late 19th century. $30

Glass butter churn mounted on an iron stand. $75

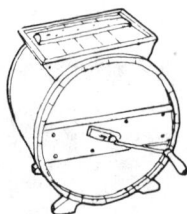

Early Victorian Scottish butter churn in pine, 48cm. high x 34cm. wide x 43cm. deep. $145

Late 19th century champion butter-churn. $225

19th century sand-blasted butter churn. $280

Revolving oak butter churn by Hathaway of Chippenham, early 20th century. $350

Victorian brown earthenware butter dish. $10

Blue and white china butter dish, circa 1890. $15

Victorian butter dish with cow, no mark. $36

Glass butter dish, cover and stand, circa 1810. $135

Brass banded oak butter dish, circa 1840. $170

One of a rare pair of early 19th century Irish cut glass butter piggins, 13cm. high. $395

Worcester oval butter tub and cover with stand, circa 1770-80, 7¼in. wide. $900

19th century Scandinavian carved and painted butter tub with flat cover, 13in. diam. $1,450

Silver revolving butter tureen, by Atkin Bros., Sheffield, 1893. $1,980

KITCHENWARE

BUTTER KNIVES

Fiddle butter knife by Jonathan Hayne, London 1825. $50

Mother-of-pearl handled butter knife by J.C., Birmingham 1853. $50

Early butter knife by Thomas Wallis, London 1798. $60

Butter knife by Richard Crasley, London 1796. $60

Thread and shell butter knife by Hayne and Cator, London 1855. $60

Butter knife by George Unite, Birmingham 1893. $70

Butter knife by Joseph Taylor, Birmingham 1790. $70

Scandinavian butter knife by G. Jensen, Copenhagen, 1960. $70

Butter knife (crested) by Edward Morley, London 1808. $70

Butter knife by Samuel Pemberton, Birmingham 1802. $75

Irish butter knife by Samuel Neville, Dublin 1810. $120

Butter knife with cast hunting scene by H. & A. Ltd., London 1917. $80

Guild of Handicrafts Ltd. silver butter knife, circa 1900, 13.5cm. long. $450

One of twenty-four George III silver gilt butter or cheese knives by Robert Garrard, London 1814.
    $1,000

Sycamore wood butter marker, circa 1830, 5in. diam. $75

19th century American wooden handleless butter stamp with incised anchor, 3½in. diam. $75

Beechwood butter marker, circa 1840, 4½in. diam. $80

19th century American wooden butter stamp carved with a running fox, 2½in. diam. $150

19th century American wooden butter stamp, carved with a cow, 3½in. diam. $150

19th century American wooden butter stamp showing a bird on a branch, 3in. diam. $225

19th century American wooden butter stamp with incised deer, 4in. diam. $300

19th century American wooden oval butter stamp with carved eagle standing on a globe, initials on either side, 5½in. long. $350

19th century American wooden butter stamp, carved with a ram, 4½in. diam. $350

CAKE STANDS

Victorian brass three-tier cakestand. $45

20th century mahogany folding cakestand. $55

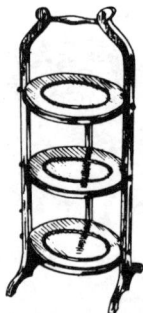

A mahogany circular, three-tier cakestand. $55

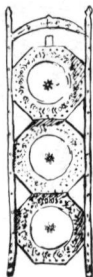

19th century inlaid hardwood folding cakestand. $60

A Victorian mahogany inlaid circular three-tier cakestand. $75

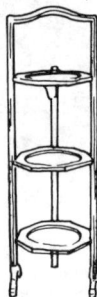

Edwardian inlaid three-tier cakestand. $80

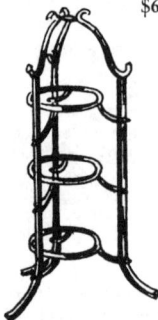

19th century brass three-tier cakestand. $105

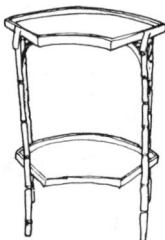

19th century pair of Japanese red lacquer fan shaped cake trays on a bamboo stand, 54cm. wide. $150

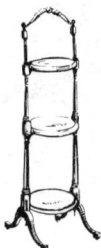

Satinwood three-tier tea table with leaf-cast bronze handle, circa 1920. $330

KITCHENWARE

CANDLE BOXES

Japanned candle box in black and red. $25

19th century brass candle holder. $55

One of two early 19th century tin candle molds, 13½in. $75

18th century elm taper box. $115

Oak candle box, circa 1790, 13in. wide. $160

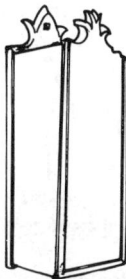

18th century oak candle box with sliding front, 16in. high. $250

American pine candle box with carved decoration on all sides, 9¾in. long. $800

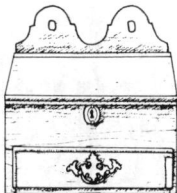

18th century American pine hanging wall candle box with double tombstone crest, 15in. wide. $800

Early 19th century Federal mahogany wall box with scrolled crest, 7¾in. wide. $1,200

KITCHENWARE

CANDLE EXTINGUISHERS

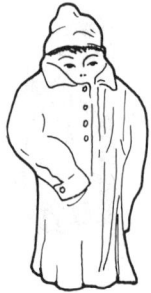

Unnamed pottery candle extinguisher. $5

Candle extinguisher by Davenport with cone-shaped stand. $35

Candle extinguisher with naturally colored face, 1885. $575

CANDLE HOLDERS

Twisted wrought iron table rushlight and candleholder on pinewood base, circa 1820, 11in. high.$130

An unusual pair of wine cellarman's candlesticks with steel stems to the top, with brass sconces and drip pans, circa 1810, 9½in. high. $190

17th century iron birdcage candleholder on tripod base, 14½in. $675

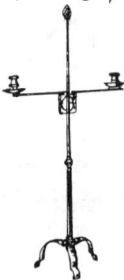

18th or 19th century Continental iron and brass standing candleholder, 63in. high. $700

One of a pair of 15th/16th century wrought iron pricket candlesticks, 19in. high. $840

Rare early 18th century turned maple lighting stand on three tapering legs, 43in. high. $2,400

KITCHENWARE

CANDLE SNUFFERS

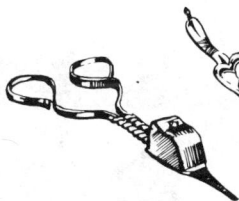

17th century bronze candle snuffer, marked with heart and cross, 6½in. long. $85

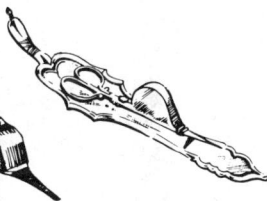

An 18th century Sicilian snuffer and stand by Pietro Donia, Messina, 11in. long, 6oz.8dwt. $370

17th century brass candle snuffer decorated with Virgin and Child, 7½in. long. $500

CANDLE STANDS

Single brass adjustable candlestick stand, the shaped lobed base covering iron weight, circa 1820, 9in. high. $110

George III mahogany adjustable candle stand on a turned base. $120

Early 18th century American pine and maple cross stretcher base candlestand, 27in. high. $425

18th century elm candlestand with circular top and splayed pine legs, 17¼in. diam. $600

Early 19th century Shaker cherry and birch candlestand, Massachusetts, 26¾in. high. $700

William and Mary candle stand in walnut with quarter veneered top and inlaid herringbone. $1,125

CANDLESTICKS

Pair of oak candlesticks
with twist stems and
brass drip pans. $20

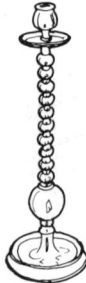

Tall brass candlestick on circular base, 18½in. high.
$45

A pair of 19th century
brass table candlesticks
on circular bases, 6½in.
high. $55

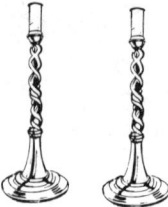

Pair of Victorian brass twist
candlesticks, 12in. high.
$70

A pair of decorated lac-
quered candlesticks,
fitted for electric light.
$90

A pair of 19th century
brass candlesticks on
octagonal bases, 12½in.
high. $125

Pair of embossed bronze
candlesticks entwined
with dragons. $135

One of a pair of 19th century brass candlesticks on
octagonal bases, 12½ins.
high. $145

Pair of mahogany table
candlesticks with fluted
stems, on circular bases,
14in. high. $165

38

KITCHENWARE

Pair of early Victorian brass candlesticks to take glass storm shades, 10½in. high. $215

One of a pair of late 19th century brass medieval revival candlesticks, 38½in. high. $295

A pair of carved walnut candlesticks, circa 1900, 18in. high. $300

One of a pair of Art Nouveau figural candlesticks, in brass plated white metal, circa 1920, 18½in. high. $325

One of a pair of English 18th century brass candlesticks, 11¾in. high. $400

One of a pair of Minton secessionist candlesticks with two loop handles, circa 1889, 52cm. high. $880

Late 19th century Flemish brass candlestick, 10.8cm. high. $820

Pair of bronze pricket candlesticks, 15th century. $3,040

Fine and rare bell-based candlestick with plain socket, circa 1600, 21cm. high. $4,950

CARDBOARD BOXES

Lever Brothers 'Sunlight Soap', circa 1890. $10

Songster needle box complete with contents. $10

Lever Brothers 'Plantol' soap, circa 1900. $15

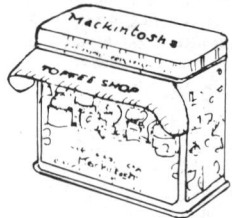

Mackintosh's toffee shop, circa 1930. $20

CARVING SETS

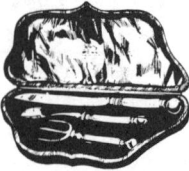

19th century plated bread knife, fork and cheese scoop with ivory handles. $45

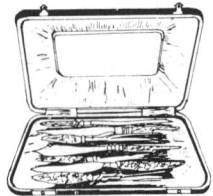

Victorian carving set with bone handles. $55

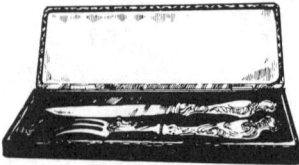

Victorian carving knife and fork with chased handles. $65

Early 18th century knife and fork, probably German, circa 1710. $395

CAULDRONS

Wood dyer's iron cauldron used as a log container, circa 1800. $125

A 16th century cast iron cooking cauldron, with original hand wrought swing handle, standing on three feet, 13in. high, 9¼in. diameter. $235

George III copper cauldron and lid, circa 1770, 22in. wide. $350

CHARGERS

18th century pewter charger with deep central bowl, 13in. diameter. $145

A large Imari charger. $540

English Delft charger with figure of William III, 13¾in. high. $1,180

CHAMBERPOTS

Decorative Victorian china chamber pot. $30

A blue and white transfer printed chamber pot, unmarked. $145

Frog chamber pot bearing the transfer portraits of Napier and the King of Abyssinia. $430

CHAMBERSTICKS

Late Victorian green enamel chamberstick. $15

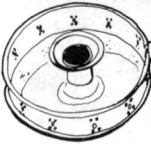

19th century brass chamberstick with handle. $15

Brass chamberstick with a drip pan. $35

Miniature ribbed pewter chamberstick with bowl-shaped drip pan, 2½in. high. $50

Victorian brass chamber candle lamp with cone snuffer. $65

Good Toleware polished chamberstick, circa 1840, 2½in. high, by H. F. & Co. $75

Sheffield plate chamberstick, circa 1810. $135

Miniature Swansea taperstick, circa 1814-22, 3in. high. $345

An early miniature pewter chamberstick, 2in. high. $350

CHAMBERSTICKS

Rare Derby chamberstick, 1760-70, 3in. high. $370

Mid 18th century copper chamberstick with pierced decoration, 7½in. long. $450

George III chamber candlestick by R. & S. Hennell, London, 1802, 10oz., 5¼in. diam. $450

George IV silver chamber candlestick, Sheffield, 1823, 8oz.15dwt. $580

Chamberlain's Worcester yellow-ground chamber candlestick with gilt leaf handle, circa 1815, 10cm. diam. $815

Silver chamberstick by Emes & Barnard, London, 1822. $980

Flight, Barr & Barr candlestick of hexagonal shape, by Barker, 4in., circa 1820-25. $1,120

Unusual George IV chamber candlestick, London, 1829, 6oz.12dwt., 4in. high. $1,350

Lowestoft blue and white candlestick. $1,755

CHEESE DISHES

Victorian floral china cheese cover. $15

Blue and white china cheese dish and cover, circa 1890. $25

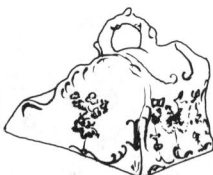

Crown Devon pottery cheese cover. $30

Large hand-painted Stilton cheese dish. $120

Large Victorian earthenware cheese dish and cover with green and brown decoration. $145

An unusual pottery cheese dish and cover, with white orange skin body and polychrome raised Japanese stylized flowers, 9in. high. $145

Large late 18th century blue and white cheese dish. $180

19th century Jasper ware Stilton dish from the Minton factory, 12in. long, 12in. high. $305

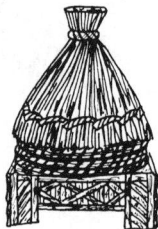

European majolica covered cheese dish, circa 1880, in the form of a grass hut, 13½in. high. $340

KITCHENWARE

CHEESE PRESSES

Mid 19th century polished steel press. $125

An interesting farmhouse cheese press, with wrought iron frame, 20in. high, circa 1800. $180

18th century hand wrought steel cheese press, complete with large brass bowl, 56in. high, circa 1720. $790

CHEESE SCOOPS

Small long-handled silver scoop, Birmingham, 1904. $35

Victorian silver cheese scoop with ivory handle. $110

Stilton cheese scoop with ejector slide, Joseph Taylor, Birmingham, 1803. $190

Irish silver cheese scoop, John Dalrymple, Dublin 1793. $225

Silver cheese scoop with ivory handle by William Ely and William Fearn, 1804, 10¼in. long. $280

Silver cheese scoop with ivory handle by TF, 1808. $325

CHESTNUT ROASTERS

Victorian polished steel chestnut roaster. $30

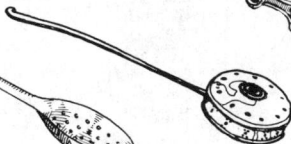

Brass circular chestnut roaster with iron handle. $55

Unusual French brass chestnut roaster with embossed lid showing an old man and a young girl. $215

KITCHENWARE

CHINA UTENSILS

19th century Wedgwood majolica fish dish. $15

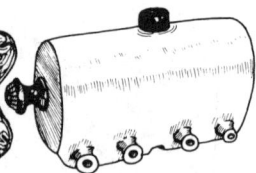

Earthenware nine position pig foster mother. $45

Stoneware ale barrel tap impressed "Doulton & Co., Lambeth, London", circa 1869. $70

One of a pair of Longton Hall cos leaf sauceboats, 7in. long. $80

Victorian decorated toilet set. $90

Small Wemyss conserve pot and cover, painted with cherries, 7.5cm. high, with matching stand. $90

Lowestoft blue and white creamboat, circa 1775, 13cm. wide. $100

Victorian portable lavatory by R. Wiss, London, in copper with a blue and white china bowl, 15in. high. $155

Blue and white lavatory pan, 'Niagara'. $170

KITCHENWARE

Royal Worcester cracker jar with squat bulbous gadrooned body, 1888, 7in. high. $175

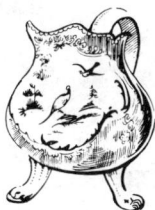

Sevres pear-shaped cream jug painted with exotic birds, circa 1755, 10cm. high. $260

Rare Glasgow saltglazed stoneware salt-kiln and cover, 14in. high. $320

Early 19th century Continental porcelain chocolate pot with angular handle, 8in. high. $350

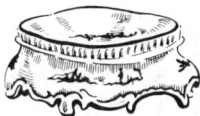

One of two Loosdrecht shaped oval quatrefoil trencher salts, circa 1770, 9.5cm. wide. $350

19th century stoneware decorated crock by Fulper Bros., Flemington, N.J., 10in. high. $350

Bow triple shell salt, 18cm. wide, circa 1760, slightly restored. $360

Late 18th century Portobello cow creamer and cover, 6¼in. long. $385

Mid 19th century American stoneware decorated water cooler with domed cover, Pennsylvania, 21½in. high. $500

47

CHINA UTENSILS

Wedgwood oviform
pepper pot with
pierced top, circa
1790, 6cm. high.
$530

One of a pair of Worces-
ter sauceboats of silver
shape, 6¾in. long, about
1755-60. $565

Chelsea strawberry leaf sauceboat with rustic handle.
$585

**Mid 18th century Mennecy
mustard pot and cover,
10cm. high. $595**

Rare mid 18th century Chan-
tilly double salt and pepper
box in three sections, 25cm.
wide. $595

Rare Wedgwood 'Queen's
ware' argyle and cover,
circa 1780-90, 6¼in. high.
$630

Bow triple salt painted
in famille rose style,
circa 1753, 13.5cm.
wide. $650

Wilkinson Ltd. 'bizarre'
lemonade set of seven
pieces, 1930's, designed
by Clarice Cliff. $720

Sevres bleu-celeste-ground
ice pail and cover, painted
with scenes of lovers after
Watteau, 25cm. high. $730

CHINA UTENSILS

One of a pair of Ridgway ice pails, covers and liners, circa 1815-20. $870

One of a pair of oval Derby two-handled Monteiths with shell handles, circa 1790, 26.5cm. wide. $915

Fine Worcester wet mustard pot, cover and spoon, 3½in. high, circa 1770. $900

Rare saltglaze porringer of small size in white, circa 1745, 4in. wide. $1,080

Ludwigsburg two-handled ecuelle, cover and stand with Ozier borders, circa 1765. $1,200

Lowestoft Pap warmer, 10¼in. high, circa 1765. $1,440

CANARIE

Rare Caughley child's guglet and basin and chamber pot en suite. $1,465

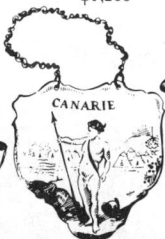

Rare Battersea bottle ticket of vine leaf form, by James Gwin and Simon-Francois Ravenet, circa 1755, 7cm. wide. $2,950

Part of a Wedgwood dinner and dessert service of one hundred and one pieces, circa 1835. $3,600

KITCHENWARE

CHOCOLATE MOLDS

An unusual chocolate
mold, possibly German,
in the shape of a lion.
$35

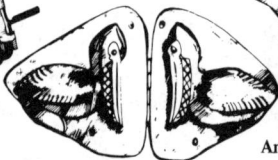

A pelican-shaped chocolate
mold, possibly German.
$35

An unusual chocolate
mold in the shape of
a dog, possibly of
German manufacture.
$35

CHOCOLATE POTS

Georgian copper choco-
late pot with fitted tur-
ned fruitwood side han-
dle, 18cm. high. $205

One of a pair of Berlin
covered chocolate pots,
7¾in. and 5½in. high,
circa 1830. $750

George III baluster chocolate pot, London, 11in.
high, 30oz.6dwt. $3,500

CLEAVERS

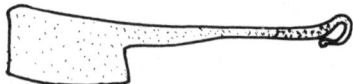

Victorian cast iron butcher's cleaver.
$20

Small Victorian chopper, with
wooden handle. $20

A butcher's small 19th century cleaver
in steel with oak handle, 13in. long.
$40

Exceptionally large old butcher's
cleaver, 26in. long. $70

CLOCKS

Victorian circular wall
clock by Jump, London.
$70

A walnut inlaid wall clock
with enameled dial.
$145

Regency mahogany
and brass inlaid wall
clock with circular
dial, 1ft.11in. high.
$170

A Victorian walnut
and floral marquetry
wall clock with
enamel dial, 75cm.
high. $180

Wall clock with circular
yew frame, painted dial
with black Roman
numerals. $190

A Victorian walnut
cased wall clock with
fluted pillars, enamel
dial and brass pendu-
lum. $260

Mahogany wall clock with
convex dial and glass.
$415

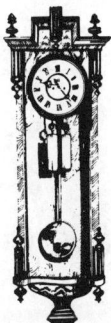

Well-figured walnut striking
Vienna regulator. $665

Oak regulator wall time-
piece, inscribed E. Howard
& Co., Boston, 31½in.
high. $1,400

51

COAL BOXES

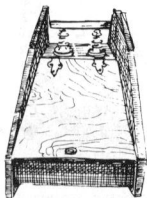

Late Victorian oak coal box with brass fittings. $65

Edwardian walnut coal cabinet with brass back-rail, handles and shovel. $65

Victorian, black japanned coal box. $80

Edwardian rosewood coal cabinet inlaid with boxwood. $90

Victorian japanned coal depot with china handle. $145

Unusual Victorian parlor coal box, 26in. high, with mirrored lid and ceramic handles. $205

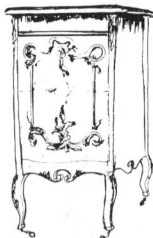

19th century mahogany serpentine fronted coal cabinet with an ormolu gallery and mounts, 1ft. 4in. wide. $260

A Pontypool coal bin. $280

French ormolu coal box, 24in. high. $360

Victorian Barge ware
coal pail. $70

19th century copper
pail with swing handle.
$75

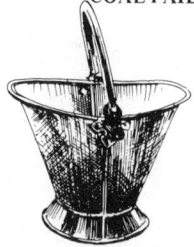

19th century copper
coal pail with a brass
handle. $75

A fine copper coal
hod with brass loop
handles, 1ft.9in.
high. $80

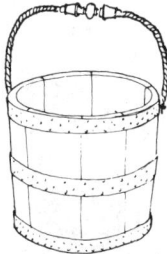

19th century stained
wood and brass
bound coal pail with
brass handle. $80

Circular copper coal
pail. $100

Copper and brass bound
oval coal pail with swing
handle. $110

Late 18th century
copper coal hod.
$125

A 19th century embossed
brass, oval coal pail, with
double hinged covers and
handle. $190

COAL SCUTTLES

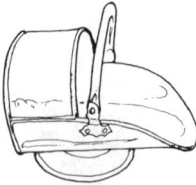

Victorian copper scoop coal scuttle with a swing handle. $75

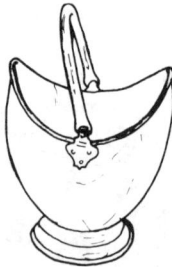

19th century brass coal helmet with a swing handle. $115

Copper helmet-shaped coal scuttle, circa 1810. $125

Copper coal scuttle with shovel. $155

A Victorian brass coal helmet, with swing handle. $170

Copper coal scuttle, circa 1800. $170

A fine Georgian copper coal scuttle with brass handle grips, 19in. long, 17in. high. $215

18th century oval copper scuttle of rare and unusual design. $280

Victorian brass coal scuttle in the form of a shell, sold with a brass coal shovel. $470

COFFEE MILLS & GRINDERS

Mid Victorian coffee grinder.
$55

Iron and wood coffee grinder, circa 1870. $100

Cast iron and brass coffee grinder, 5in. square.
$125

A large 19th century iron and brass tub wheel coffee mill. $215

A rare, polished iron coffee bean roaster, circa 1760. $215

A fine Victorian brass and steel coffee grinder, 26in. high. $295

Coffee merchant's grinder with original paintwork, 27in. high. $450

18th century oak coffee mill, 7¼in. high, with brass mounted grinder handle. $620

Dutch or French walnut coffee mill, early 18th century, 6½in. high.
$1,450

KITCHENWARE

COFFEE POTS

Porzellan-Manufaktur-Burgau porcelain coffee pot, 20cm. high, circa 1910. $160

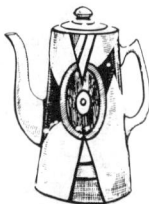

Newport pottery 'bizarre' coffee pot, designed by Clarice Cliff, 1930's, 19cm. high. $200

Meissen baluster coffee pot and cover with knob finial, circa 1770, 24.5cm. high. $370

Staffordshire glazed redware conical miniature coffee pot and cover, circa 1755, 16.5cm. high. $470

Qianlong famille rose cafe-au-lait ground slender conical coffee pot and shallow domed cover, 27.5cm. high. $750

Large Staffordshire coffee pot, circa 1825, 11in. high, with C-scrolled handle. $800

Whieldon coffee pot and cover, 7¼in. high, circa 1750. $900

Rare Derby blue and white coffee pot and cover, 8¾in. high, about 1765-80. $900

George III vase-shaped coffee pot, 11in. high, Edinburgh, 1802, 25oz. 14dwt. $1,015

George IV coffee pot, 8¾in. high, by Joseph Angell, London, 1828, 28oz.7dwt. $1,025

George III circular coffee pot by George Ashforth & Co., Sheffield, 1802, 9in. high. $1,060

Victorian oval tapering coffee pot by J. Whipple & Co., Exeter, 1877, 27oz., 9¼in. high. $1,130

Hochst coffee pot and cover with branch handle, 24cm. high, circa 1755-65. $1,175

George III Scottish coffee pot by Ker & Dempster, Edinburgh, 1763. $1,440

Volkstedt coffee pot and cover with pear-shaped body, circa 1760-65, 20cm. high. $1,790

French Empire vase-shaped coffee pot, Paris, circa 1800, 26.3cm. high, 840gm. $2,025

George III coffee pot on stand by Paul Storr, London, 1802, 12¾in. high, 55oz. $3,860

Bottger Meissen red stoneware coffee pot, circa 1715, 14.5cm. high. $6,900

CORKSCREWS

Pocket boxwood cork-screw and holder. $15

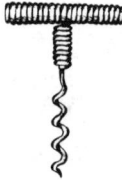

Unusual twist spring steel corkscrew. $20

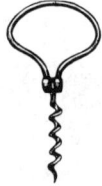

Large pocket folding steel corkscrew. $20

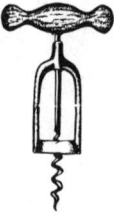

19th century iron cork-screw with wooden handle. $20

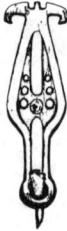

Crown cork remover.$25

Victorian corkscrew with horn handle and brush, about 1860. $35

Johnnie Walker Scotch advertising corkscrew with brush handle. $40

Lignum vitae corkscrew with brush handle. $40

Georgian pocket steel corkscrew and holder. $55

Fine 19th century iron corkscrew with brush handle. $55

Steel sprung corkscrew. $65

19th century iron corkscrew with ivory handle. $65

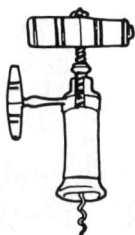

19th century Plum's patent ratchet corkscrew with ivory handle, brass barrel and steel screw. $90

Rare bright steel folding pocket corkscrew, circa 1830. $100

Wine taster's tap screw with brush handle. $100

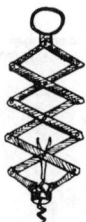

Wier's patent corkscrew of 1884, single form. $105

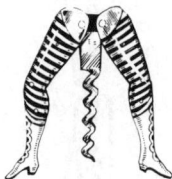

German pocket corkscrew in the form of a can-can dancers legs. $125

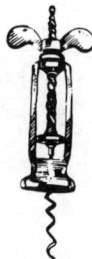

Unusual Victorian brass corkscrew. $125

CORKSCREWS

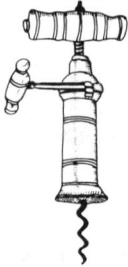

A Dowler's type corkscrew. $145

A Victorian wood and steel corkscrew. $175

Victorian brass and ivory corkscrew. $180

Impressive Victorian brass and cast iron bar corkscrew with beechwood handle, 12in. high. $200

Victorian brass and ivory corkscrew. $205

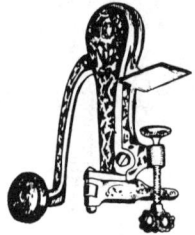

Fine 19th century bar corkscrew, cast iron with round knob wooden handle, 9in. high. $215

19th century cast iron bar corkscrew with round knob wooden handle. $215

J. H. Perille's patent single side lever corkscrew. $275

Excelsior Lever simple corkscrew. $350

CORKSCREWS

Unusual brass Victorian corkscrew. $360

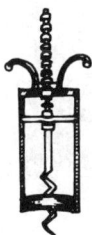

Early steel corkscrew. $395

Late 18th century example of the first patented corkscrew in this country. $405

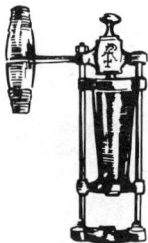

Steel rack and pinion hand corking device, 6¼in. high. $620

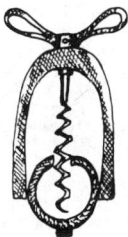

Rare corkscrew marked Bonsa. $680

Charles Hull, 1864 patent, single lever corkscrew. $730

Rare direct pressure corkscrew, unmarked. $750

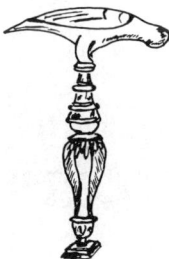

Dutch silver corkscrew by Hendrik Smook, Amsterdam, 1753. $1,465

Mid 19th century French bronze corkscrew. $3,150

CRUETS

Late 19th century four-bottle plated cruet.
$90

A Cunerville sauceboat with two jugs. $90

American amberina castor set, circa 1890, in plated silver frame. $350

George IV silver cruet stand with glass bottles.
$400

Late 19th century Dresden yellow-ground cruet, fitted with two ewers and covers, 23cm. high.
$495

Late 18th century Leeds creamware cruet stand and bottles, 11in. high.
$520

George III cruet frame with pierced gallery sides, by John Delmester, 1764, 16.25oz. $615

Wedgwood creamware cruet with five containers, circa 1810, 17cm. wide.
$690

Wedgwood creamware cruet painted by Emile Lessore, circa 1865, 22cm. high. $1,060

CRUETS

Parcel gilt egg cruet of six, by R. Hennell & Sons, London, 1850, 27.9oz.
$1,135

George IV four-bottle cruet frame by Paul Storr, London, 1824. $1,240

Hukin & Heath silver cruet in carrying frame, 1881, designed by Christopher Dresser, 14.25cm. high.
$1,240

Rare set of enameled 'mock china' cruet bottles, circa 1760, 4¾in. to 7¼in. high.
$2,250

Table cruet by Paul Storr, London, 1811, 30oz.
$3,040

George IV four-bottle cruet frame by Philip Rundell, London, 1820, 43oz.15dwt., 11in. high. $3,220

A pair of Louis XVI two-bottle cruets, 12¾in. wide, by Jacques Favre, Paris, 1778, 51oz.1dwt.
$3,825

63

CUPS & SAUCERS

Staffordshire willow
pattern cup and
saucer, circa 1860.
$15

Victorian cranberry glass
custard cup. $25

Famille rose coffee
cup and saucer
decorated with
flowers. $30

Early 19th century porce-
lain cup and saucer,
painted with flowers.
$35

Royal Worcester teacup and
saucer. $45

Lowestoft tea bowl
and saucer decorated
in the Chinese style.
$115

Antique brass loving cup
with handles copper riv-
eted to body, circa 1850,
9in. high. $125

Sevres coffee cup and
saucer with paintings of
landscapes and birds,
circa 1760. $175

Moorcroft loving cup of
broad cylindrieal shape,
flaring at rim, signed, 19cm.
high. $215

KITCHENWARE

Elers redware coffee cup and saucer, circa 1760. $225

Early Worcester fluted coffee cup, 1752-54. $250

Sevres style chocolate cup, cover and stand painted with entwined flowering foliage. $340

Early 19th century Pinxton cup and saucer painted with a landscape medallion. $350

19th century Berlin cup and saucer. $450

'Marriage Pattern' coffee cup, teacup and saucer of fluted form, circa 1775. $465

Swansea teacup, coffee cup and saucer, 1814-22. $540

Rare early posset cup, 3½in. high, circa 1690. $565

Longton Hall tea bowl and saucer, circa 1750. $620

65

CUTLERY BOXES

Victorian country made
oak knife box. $35

Georgian mahogany
knife box, with brass
carrying handle.
$100

Mahogany and satinwood
oblong cutlery tray, 2ft. x
6½in. $160

Canteen of Old English pattern table cutlery by Martin
Hall & Co., Sheffield, in oak
case. $350

Hepplewhite cherrywood
cutlery box, 14in. long,
circa 1820. $450

Sheraton mahogany
knifebox of square
tapering form with
ebony and boxwood
stringing, 55cm. high.
$630

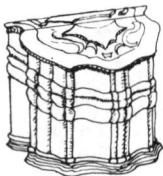

18th century Portu-
guese padoukwood
cutlery box. $1,180

Pair of Sheraton period
cutlery urns.
$1,575

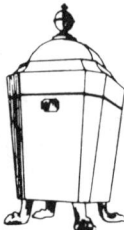

Canteen of cutlery for
twelve persons.
$1,500

CUTLERY URNS

Late 18th century George III cutlery urn of ovoid form in mahogany with boxwood and ebony lines, 27in. high. $315

One of a pair of mahogany cutlery vases in George III style, 28in. high. $360

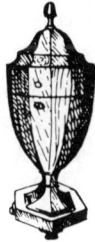

Georgian mahogany urn fully fitted for cutlery. $485

Late 18th century urn-shaped mahogany knife box. $765

George III satinwood cutlery urn with stepped lid, circa 1790, 2ft.4in. high. $965

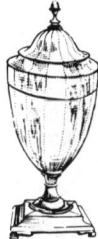

George III satinwood cutlery urn, 28in. high, circa 1785. $970

One of a pair of 'George III' mahogany knife urns with gadrooned lids, circa 1880. $1,150

Late 18th century Sheraton period cutlery urn. $1,370

One of a pair of George III mahogany cutlery urns, 2ft.4in. high, circa 1790. $2,590

DECANTER BOXES

'Swiss Chalet' decanter case with hinged roof, circa 1900, 25½in. wide. $105

Small early 19th century mahogany decanter box containing four decanters. $170

Georgian mahogany decanter set with six Venetian gilt decorated spirit decanters, circa 1795. $340

A George III satinwood and kingwood banded decanter box, the lid and front inlaid with shields, 7in. wide. $340

Coromandel and brass mounted liquor casket fitted with four cut glass decanters. $405

Inlaid case with four decanters and nine glasses. $455

19th century rosewood traveling drinks cabinet. $475

'Directore' mahogany decanter box, 19½in. high, circa 1912. $700

Early 19th century mahogany and brass bound decanter case, 22cm. wide. $730

KITCHENWARE

DECANTER BOXES

Mid 19th century English kingwood and mother-of-pearl bombe liqueur cabinet, 11 x 13½in. $1,015

Boulle and ebonized rosewood serpentine decanter box with glasses, 13in. wide, circa 1850. $1,025

George III mahogany decanter box, fully fitted. $1,015

Oak decanter box by H.H. Dobson & Sons, London, circa 1850, 9¾in. long. $1,240

Superb cased set of nine late 17th century cordial or spirit clear glass bottles in a wrought iron banded oak case, circa 1690. $1,350

Early 18th century Austro-Hungarian octagonal casket containing twelve gilt decorated glass bottles, 26.5cm. wide. $1,675

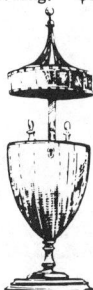

One of a pair of late Victorian mahogany urn-shaped decanter boxes, 31in. high. $1,835

Traveling decanter case with glasses and decanters. $1,915

Unusual parquetry table decanter set with globe body, circa 1860-80, 13¼in. high. $2,920

KITCHENWARE

DISHES

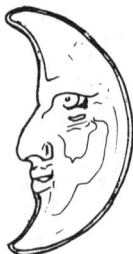

Brass 'Man in the Moon' dish, circa 1905. $25

German sweetmeat dish divided into six sections with ruffled rim, 10¼in. wide. $50

Minton sardine dish and cover decorated in polychrome, 23.5cm. wide. $90

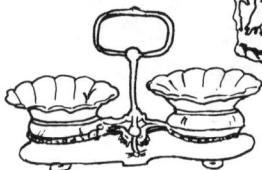

Victorian ruby glass double bon bon dish in a plated stand. $100

Victorian earthenware game dish. $125

Chelsea leaf dish, circa 1758, 28cm. wide. $170

Rare late 18th century American commemorative earthenware dish, 14¾in. diam. $235

18th century glass sweetmeat dish on tripod scroll feet, 6.5cm. high. $250

Liberty & Co. pewter muffin dish and cover by Archibald Knox, circa 1905, 29cm. wide. $300

KITCHENWARE

Liverpool delft sweetmeat dish, 8¼in., about 1750. $405

Chelsea leaf dish molded as two lettuce leaves, circa 1755, 25.5cm. wide. $450

WMF silvered metal Art Nouveau dish, 47cm. wide, circa 1900. $450

A Chelsea 'silver shape' dish with brown edged wavy rim, 11½in. wide, 1752-54. $475

Unusual sweetmeat dish, with double ogee bowl, 7in. high, circa 1760. $520

One of a pair of Chelsea kidney-shaped dishes, 11in. $675

Late 18th century slipware baking dish with a trellis design, 14½in. wide. $720

Staffordshire covered vegetable dish with high domed cover, circa 1825, 12¼in. long. $750

Bristol leaf-shaped pickle dish from Benjamin Lund's factory, 1749-51, 10cm. wide. $2,765

71

DOMESTIC IMPLEMENTS

Miniature bone-cased tape
measure. $10

Painted metal stamp.
                  $15

Victorian stoneware
hot water bottle.$15

American, Dover pattern
whisk, in iron, circa 1904.
          $15

Georgian brass shoe horn.
          $30

Late 19th century hour
glass egg timer in Mauchlin
stand. $30

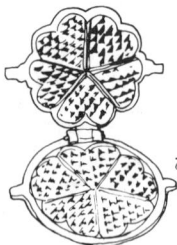

Victorian waffle iron.
          $35

Edwardian set of ivory cocktail sticks. $35

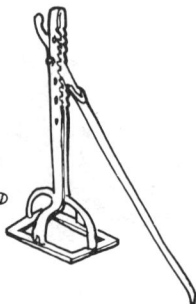

Adjustable iron cart jack,
19th century. $35

19th century beadwork tea cosy. $35

Victorian brass and copper horse mane singer. $35

Victorian cast iron boot scraper. $45

Silver Art Nouveau button hook with Birmingham made handle. $45

Victorian plated egg steamer. $55

Hand carved beech grain shovel. $55

19th century beechwood smoothing plane, 7¼in. long. $65

Brass cased set of three steel fleams, circa 1820, 3½in. long. $65

Saltglaze stoneware Cyder dispensing jar, 18in. high, with pewter spigot.$65

73

KITCHENWARE

DOMESTIC IMPLEMENTS

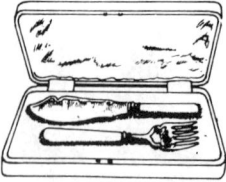

Cased set of Victorian silver servers. $65

2½ gallon iron fountain. $65

Georgian silver framed spectacles by E. T., London, 1823. $70

One of a pair of unusual brass and copper shaving mugs. $75

A brass and steel desk knife sharpener, with steel roller supports on pillars, circa 1825, 5½in. long, 4in. deep and 3½in. high. $90

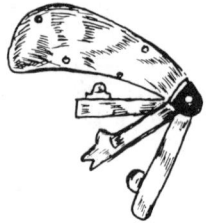

Brass and cow horn pocket fleam, circa 1820. $95

Scandinavian carved and painted mangling board, circa 1803, 26¼in. long. $100

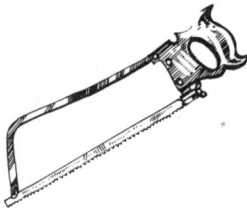

19th century butcher's bone saw, 23in. long. $100

Fisherman's fine salmon gaff, 16½in. long, circa 1840. $100

KITCHENWARE

DOMESTIC IMPLEMENTS

Rare circular brass tripod candle reflector, circa 1800, 4½in. diam. $105

Late 19th century adjustable hat stretcher of walnut and cast iron, 13in. high. $110

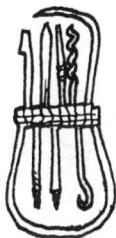

Near Eastern copper charcoal burner of circular form with pierced domed cover and brass loop handles, 47cm. diam. $170

Huntsman's cut steel pocket tool kit with eight folding tools, circa 1820. $170

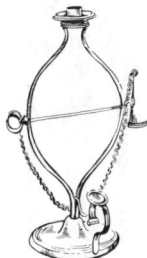

19th century mahogany bootrack. $170

Copper brewer's yeast vessel with loop handle and long pouring spout, circa 1890, 10in. high. $200

Silver plated wax jack with reeded base and nozzle, 6¾in. high. $230

Liberty & Co. silver stopper by Archibald Knox, Birmingham, 1906, 6.5cm. high. $260

Very rare three arched cast iron fireback, dated 1630, 23in. wide. $280

DOMESTIC IMPLEMENTS

Silver plated Victorian triple shell biscuit warmer. $310

Large copper and brass hot punch dispenser, complete with burner, 20in. high, circa 1840. $305

Early 18th century American wrought iron pipe kiln, 13½in. long. $350

Solid rosewood embroidery frame with trestle supports, circa 1850, 48in. wide. $400

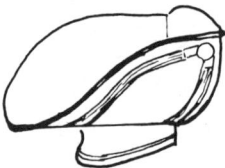

One of a pair of grocer's display scuttles decorated in red and gold, circa 1820. $530

Late 18th century water cistern with tap, 9in. high. $495

Mid 19th century Spanish chestnut warmer with brass charger, 39½in. diam. $680

One of a pair of George IV boot jacks by Paul Storr, 7½in. long, London 1825. $720

18th century Spanish wrought iron well head with lily finial, 72in. high. $800

Kalliope musical Christmas tree stand, 59cm. wide, circa 1900. $875

Four-place motorist's picnic service in black fabric case. $960

George III silver wax jack by J. Langford and J. Sebille, London, 1764, 5½in. high, 8¼oz. $1,080

Unusual Martin, Hall & Co. silver spoon warmer in the shape of a lady's shoe, Sheffield, 1898, 534gm. $1,230

Early 19th century decanting cradle. $1,364

Jensen cocktail shaker designed by Harold Nielsen, in three sections, 28cm. high, 1930's.
$1,405

18th century German pewter wasserbehalter by Georg Ludwig Ruepprecht, Memmingen, 12½in. high.
$1,465

White enamel bath with chromium plated super-structure, circa 1900.
$2,720

Rare Louis XV Royal brass mounted copper wall cistern and bowl, late 18th century, 2ft. high. $8,440

DOMESTIC MACHINES

Late 19th century Enterprise meat chopper. $20

Late 19th century iron raisin stoner. $45

Early 20th century English marmalade chopper. $55

Victorian iron cherry seeder. $55

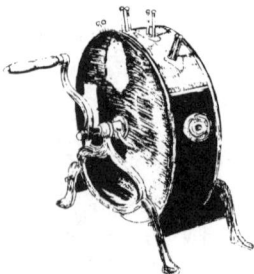

Late Victorian knife cleaner. $90

Cast iron and brass Victorian mincer by Burgess & Key, 13 x 6in. $115

Copper fire extinguisher with five oval brass plaques, 1930, 29in. high. $125

Mid 19th century French mechanical roasting jack in brass and sheet iron. $150

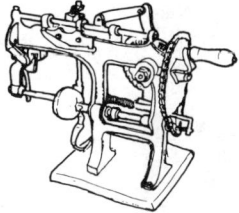

Electric fan heater, designed by Wells Coates, 1930's, 29.5cm. high. $195

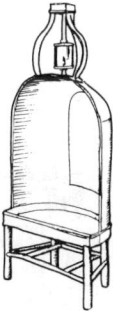

Apple corer made around 1890-1910, works on the same principle as a sewing machine. $280

Hastener in sheet iron with a brass bottle-jack above, 1880, 370cm. high x 155cm. wide x 99cm. deep. $370

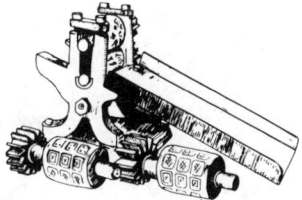

English sweet-making machine in cast iron, with brass scoop and copper pan, circa 1880's. $420

DOOR FURNITURE

Pair of 18th century brass door handles. $25

A bronze classical female head door mount with bas-relief vines. $25

Art Nouveau bronze door handle, 35cm. long. $45

Victorian cast iron door knocker, circa 1850, 8in. high. $45

Finely detailed Adam period door knocker, 9in. high. $95

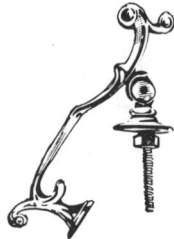

Antique brass door knocker, 8in. high, with circular brass plate. $110

Late 19th century French bronze door knocker, 11¾in. high. $115

Bronze door knocker, by Onslow E. Whiting, 13in. high, circa 1900. $340

Early 17th century Venetian bronze door knocker, 16in. high. $1,465

DOOR LOCKS

George III brass door lock, 7in. wide, with keeper and key. $135

Brass and steel penny lavatory lock, circa 1870. $135

17th century engraved door lock and key. $145

French steel-cased door lock with heavy ormolu trim, brass handles and escutcheon plate, circa 1790. $225

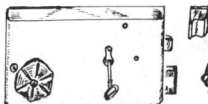

19th century Queen Anne design brass door lock. $260

Louis XVI ormolu door lock in working order, complete with key. $340

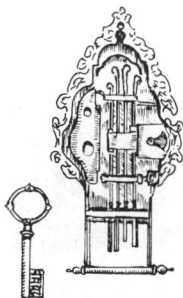

Late 17th century German door lock with brass finials. $450

Late 17th century German door lock in iron, 13in. long, with original key. $1,240

16th century steel door lock with key, from the Bohemia's Castle of Dux, where Casanova's body was finally laid to rest, 19½in. wide. $1,410

81

DOOR STOPS

A solid cast brass standing plaque, stamped on back 'Crowley & Co., Manchester', circa 1860, 9in. long, 7in. high. $45

Victorian brass dog door poster. $55

Victorian cast iron door stop, 9in. high. $55

19th century cast iron door stop depicting a rampant lion. $65

Victorian cast iron door stop of a horse, on a stepped base, 11¼in. long, 10in. high. $75

A 19th century brass dolphin door stopper. $110

A good cast iron figure of a horse, standing on a modeled base, 1ft.8in. long. $115

A historical cast brass door stop of King George IV leaning on a pillar, 7½in. long, 8in. high. $115

One of a pair of heavy cast iron door stops of zebras, circa 1820, 10½in. long, 8in. high. $180

ETUIS

Ebony oval etui case with recesses for scissors, etc., in French hallmarked gold and silver. $260

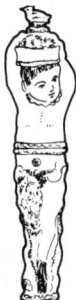

Etui and scent bottle modeled as a putto. $270

An unusual late 19th century book-shaped etui of tortoiseshell, ivory and silver, with a sliding end covering two inner containers. $270

An etui depicting a girl holding a basket, circa 1756. $340

Mid 18th century jasper and gold mounted etui. $370

Chelsea etui with harlequin head top, 12½in., circa 1760. $520

Late 18th century Staffordshire etui complete with thimble, needles and scissors. $1,215

A rare 'Girl in a Swing' etui with Columbine head top, circa 1754. $2,125

Louis XV gold etui by Jean Ducrollay of Paris, 1745-50. $9,565

83

FENDERS

Late 19th century wrought iron half circle fender, 2ft.4in. wide. $65

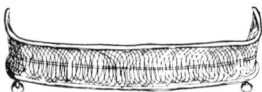

Victorian pierced brass fender. $110

Victorian cast iron fender. $145

Victorian brass fender, 4ft.6in. wide. $145

Victorian pierced brass fender on paw feet, 4ft.6in. wide. $165

George III serpentine pierced fender in polished steel, circa 1800, 36in. long. $185

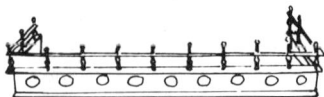

Victorian brass fender with rail, 177cm. wide. $215

Magnificent 19th century polished steel and brass fender. $630

Rare 19th century bronze fire curb with pierced center panel, 62½in. long. $690

English, shaped front brass club fender, with lion mask and green leather studded seats, circa 1865. $810

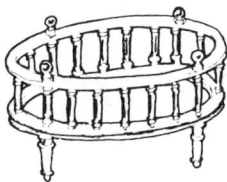

An iron basket
grate, 2ft. wide.
$135

William IV period cast
iron hob grate, circa 1830,
26in. wide. $190

Antique cast iron front to
a hob grate, with brass
knobs, apron and side
panels, 25½in. wide, circa
1840. $215

Cast iron and brass dog
grate, circa 1890.
$290

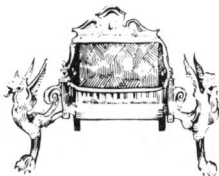

Early 19th century fire grate
with brass mounts, 2ft.6in.
wide. $385

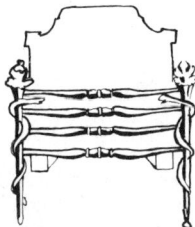

Regency period brass
basket grate, 1ft.10in.
wide. $540

Adam style fire grate,
34in. wide. $820

An attractive polished
steel fire grate, standing
on two Adam style tap-
ering fluted legs, with
urns surmounting each
one, circa 1790.$1,000

George III paktong fire
grate of Adam design,
35in. wide.$4,320

FIREDOGS

Victorian iron and brass firedogs. $35

Pair of 18th century andirons. $75

One of a pair of brass fire iron rests, by Christopher Dresser, 1880's, 21.75cm. wide. $80

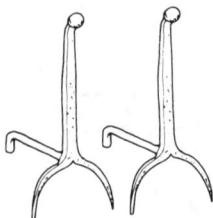

Wrought iron andirons, circa 1710, 16in. high. $135

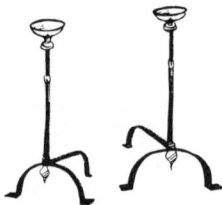

18th century pair of French steel and brass cresset spit dogs, 28in. high. $200

One of a pair of late 17th/ early 18th century brass andirons with downswept supports and ball feet, 18½in. high. $375

One of a pair of early 19th century American Federal brass George Washington figural andirons, 21in. high. $500

Renaissance style brass andirons on curved legs, 82cm. high. $525

One of a pair of mid 18th century Dutch brass andirons, 1ft.5½in. high. $640

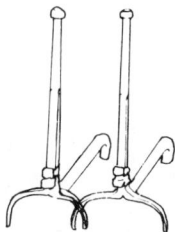

An exceptionally fine pair
of hand wrought firedogs
of Elizabeth I period, with
spit hooks, 29in. high,
circa 1570. $810

One of a pair of mid 18th
century Chippendale bell
metal andirons, 20in. high.
$1,000

A pair of late 18th cen-
tury American brass and-
irons, 25in. high. $1,000

Pair of large mid 19th century bronze firedogs.
$1,125

Pair of early 19th century
Federal brass and wrought
iron steeple-top andirons,
21in. high. $1,150

One of a pair of Louis XVI
ormolu chenets on leaf-cast
plinths, 1ft. high.
$1,520

One of a pair of late 17th
century Italo-Flemish
bronze andirons, 18½in.
high. $2,700

One of a pair of 17th century Venetian bronze andirons, 72.5cm. high.
$3,455

One of a pair of ormolu
chenets of Louis XV
period. $3,600

FIRESCREENS

Late 19th century pressed brass fire screen. $45

19th century brass fireguard, 3ft.6in. wide. $65

Victorian mirror fire screen hand-painted with roses. $65

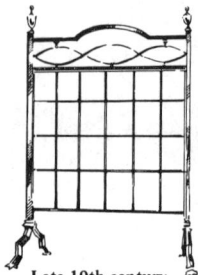

Late 19th century brass and glass firescreen. $65

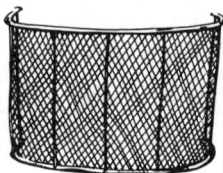

19th century brass fireguard. $65

Victorian brass firescreen with painted decoration. $80

Art Deco brass sparkguard carved with a peacock. $90

Two-fold bamboo firescreen with painted glass panels. $90

Regency satinwood and rosewood inlaid pole fire screen with embroidered panel, on splay support, 4ft.4in. high. $210

Mid 19th century rosewood adjustable screen with tapestry, 36in. high. $225

Mahogany pole screen with brass stem, base with cabriole legs, circa 1860, 60½in. high. $380

Late 19th century American stained glass firescreen with brass frame, 24in. wide. $425

Stained glass firescreen with painted central panel, circa 1880, 32in. high. $425

John Pearson bronze and wrought iron firescreen, circa 1906, 27½in. high. $450

Mid 19th century gilt bronze fire guard, 66cm. high. $520

Walnut firescreen, central panel showing a mother and three children, circa 1860, 33in. wide. $650

Giltwood and stained glass screen, circa 1900, 62in. wide. $1,015

American leaded glass firescreen, circa 1900, 45¼in. high. $3,825

89

FIRE SURROUNDS

A black and red veined mantelpiece, with cast iron fireplace. $180

Barnard, Bishop & Barnard cast brass fireplace surround, 1873, 45.2cm. wide. $390

Mid 19th century cast iron mantelpiece with cavetto cornice, 74in. wide. $410

A pine mantelpiece with carved rosettes and beadwork and partly fluted, inside measurements, 39 x 39in. $385

Carved oak combined mantelpiece and overmantel, 70in. wide. $680

Late 18th century French carved walnut fire surround, 40in. high. $720

A 19th century pine fire surround, of classical design, with applied gesso floral swags to center panel, 59 x 54½ x 9in. $715

Mason's ironstone fireplace surround, the side pillars in blue, with colored flowers in relief, 65in. wide. $1,890

Early George III pine chimneypiece with later carved shelf, 66in. wide. $6,765

KITCHENWARE

FIRE IRONS

A set of three fire
implements with
Adam style handles.
$100

Early 19th century
brass fire irons com-
plete with matching
stand. $145

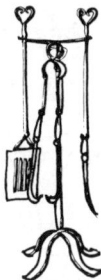

A fine set of polished steel
fire irons on a stand, circa
1840. $160

FIRESIDE CRANES

Late 18th century iron fireside crane with pot hook.
$80

Early 18th century wrought
iron chimney crane, 29¼in.
long. $190

Fireside crane with two
hinges, 26½in. lcng,
circa 1730, initialled S.
W. $200

FISH PANS

Victorian copper
chafing dish, 13in.
wide. $70

A large oval copper salmon
pan with brass loop handles.
$90

An early copper fish
kettle and lid with
bell metal carrying
handles, 20in. wide.
$190

FISH SLICES

Pair of late 19th century fish servers with bone handles, circa 1880. $60

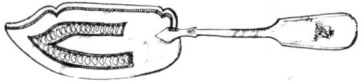

Silver fish slice by I. S., 1807. $100

Silver fish slice by John, Henry and Charles Lias, 1848, 12in. long. $125

Fiddle-pattern fish slice by Jonathan Hayne, 1834, 12in. long, 5oz. $200

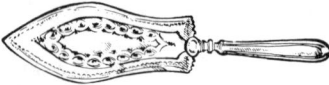

Silver fish slice by Peter and Ann Bateman, 1798. $400

Pair of Harrison Bros. & Howson fish servers, Sheffield, 1865, in fitted case. $475

Fish slice by Faberge, Moscow, 1898-1908, with monogrammed handle. $785

Silver fish trowel by Richard Williams, 1770, 13in. long. $900

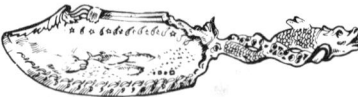

Cast silver fish slice by William Trayes, 1837, 7oz.14dwt. $1,240

18th century Dutch fish slice, 4oz. 14dwt. $1,485

18th century Dutch serving slice, 15¼in. long, by Wm. Pont, Amsterdam, 1772, 6oz.14dwt. $1,685

18th century Dutch fish slice, by Jan Diederik Pont, 1760, 15in. long, 6oz.15dwt. $2,590

KITCHENWARE

Small Victorian pewter flask, 3½in. diam. $10

Pressed glass flask, 7½in. high, cork insert for stopper, about 1896. $25

Stoneware spirit flask molded on each side to show Rice, an American entertainer, 8in. high. $180

Stoneware spirit flask, depicting Daniel O'Connell. $305

Mid 18th century Armorial middle-European enameled glass flask, with pewter rim, 16.8cm. high. $360

German enameled flask with pewter mounted neck, 12.5cm. high. $500

19th century South German hexagonal pewter canister, 13in. high. $600

Late 18th century German flask, 8¾in. high, in pewter. $1,100

German enameled flask with pewter mounted neck, 17.5cm. high. $1,145

93

FOOTMEN

A steel kettle stand, with brass handles and cabriole legs. $70

A small George II steel footman, 13½in. x 10½in. $90

George II steel footman with five 1in. flat slats across the top, standing on cabriole front legs, circa 1740, 18½in. wide, 12in. deep, 13½in. high. $125

Unusual copper, steel and brass cabriole leg footman with a single drawer. $180

19th century brass footman, pierced with cabriole shaped front supports, 12½in. high. $185

19th century footman with griddle. $190

Cast and wrought iron footman, circa 1820, 12in. long. $235

Late 18th century brass tavern footman. $270

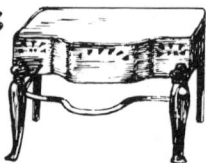

Pierced brass George III footman with handles. $270

Victorian bread fork with wooden handle. $10

Silver pickle fork with ivory handle, about 1820. $25

Silver butter fork, Sheffield, 1865. $20

Silver salmon fork with bone handle, late Victorian. $25

A polished steel steak fork with turned screw type handle, circa 1840, 24in. long. $35

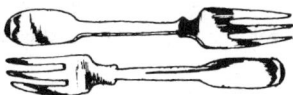

Pair of George IV pickle forks, 4½in. long, Dublin 1824, by M. West. $90

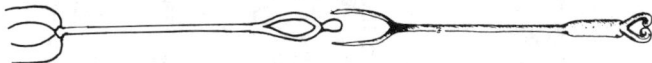

Four prong 28in. long steel steak fork, circa 1710. $125

17th century steel steak fork, ram's horn top, circa 1660. $125

Pair of 18th century oyster forks, Old English thread. $135

Silver six-pronged serving fork, Simon Harris, London, 1808. $250

One of a set of twelve three-prong table forks, by Wm. Wooler, London, 1764, 28oz. $595

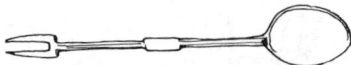

17th century silver sucket fork with rat tail bowl, by T A., London 1690. $700

Rare, early 17th century French two prong fork. $1,500

One of two Louis XIV three prong forks by Matthurin Villian, Paris, 1677. $2,500

FURNITURE
CHAIRS

19th century bentwood chair. $30

19th century child's chair in elm. $35

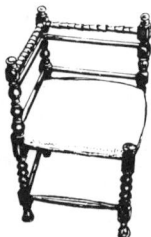

An ebonized corner chair, the seat covered in green velour. $80

A 20th century rush-seated oak elbow chair. $80

Victorian mahogany capstan chair with leather seat. $80

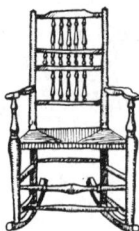

Spindle-backed 19th century rocking chair with rush seat. $90

Late Victorian elm smoker's chair on turned legs with double H-stretcher. $100

Elm high ladder back armchair with rush seat. $110

19th century carver with rush seat. $115

CHAIRS

FURNITURE

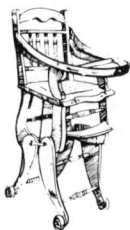

19th century child's high chair with tray and foot rest. $125

Late 18th century Windsor stick-back armchair in elm, ash and beech, with crinoline stretchers. $125

Country armchair in elm. $145

Antique ladder back rush-seated open armchair. $170

19th century elm high back Windsor chair with turned legs and stretcher. $230

Antique high winged comb back chair with saddle seat. $270

Late 18th century Windsor armchair in elm, ash and beech, with shaped pierced splat. $290

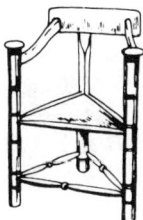

18th century elmwood corner chair with turned supports. $290

One of six Art & Crafts oak side chairs, Gustav Stickley, New York, circa 1912. $300

97

FURNITURE
CHAIRS

Small early 19th century comb-back chair on turned legs. $335

18th century yewwood low back Windsor chair with pierced splat and elm seat. $355

Early 20th century fruitwood armchair, by E. Gimson. $380

18th century comb-back elbow chair with shaped toprail. $565

Mid 18th century American fan back Windsor side chair, 36in. high. $585

One of a set of three thumb back side chairs, signed H. Cook, New England, circa 1820. $650

18th century American ladder back armchair, 46in. high. $685

One of a set of six stained beechwood North Country chairs, mid 19th century. $695

19th century Scandinavian carved and painted armchair on spiral supports. $700

98

CHAIRS

FURNITURE

One of a set of six mid 19th century unusual country-made chairs with spade-shaped backs, restored. $735

17th century primitive comb-back chair with elmwood seat. $730

George I oak armchair with panelled back, dated 1723. $730

Mid 18th century knuckle arm Windsor chair with bow back and bobbin turned stretchers. $825

East Anglican oak wainscot chair, circa 1700. $845

One of a set of seven ladder back chairs with original rush seats re-seated in seagrass. $970

One of six antique elm Windsor stick back armchairs with crinoline stretchers. $1,330

High back yewwood Windsor armchair with crinoline stretcher. $1,395

One of a pair of early 19th century Windsor armchairs. $3,150

FURNITURE
CUPBOARDS

Victorian stripped pine corner cupboard with glazed doors. $110

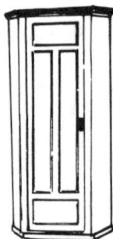

19th century white-painted pine corner cupboard, 2.11 m. high. $180

A carved oak corner cupboard the panel door with inlaid motifs of shells. $280

George III pinewood corner cupboard. $440

Late 18th century mahogany hanging corner cupboard. $450

Late 18th century oak corner cupboard with paneled doors. $575

Late 18th century oak standing corner cupboard with plain pediment, 4ft.3in. wide. $680

A fine 18th century oak livery cupboard, handles not original, 72in. high. $1,080

Early 18th century oak cupboard, 55in. wide. $1,125

CUPBOARDS

FURNITURE

Late 18th century American Chippendale basswood corner cupboard, 45in. wide. $1,400

17th century carved oak court cupboard. $1,465

Early Louis XV provincial oak cupboard, 3ft.10in. wide, circa 1730. $1,845

Georgian oak bacon cupboard on bracket feet. $1,915

Antique Flemish carved oak cupboard, 5ft.4in. wide. $2,250

Massive oak cupboard, 16th century, 49½in. wide, 66in. high. $2,340

18th century oak court cupboard, 56½in. wide. $2,475

A late 17th century oak tridarn, 53in. wide. $2,735

17th century South German walnut and inlaid side cupboard. $4,275

FURNITURE
DRESSERS

Small Victorian stripped pine dresser base with shaped brass handles, 4ft. wide. $315

18th century French provincial oak buffet, 124cm. wide. $360

A carved oak dresser, the drawers in the frieze with carved lion mask handles, 4ft. wide. $450

Late Victorian pine dresser. $565

Victorian carved oak dresser with pot board. $565

Early 20th century oak dresser with brass handles. $565

19th century Jacobean style dresser, 4ft.7in. wide. $675

Late 19th century walnut Continental dresser. $675

Small 19th century stripped pine dresser with drawers and cupboards, 3ft.3in. wide. $785

DRESSERS   **FURNITURE**

An early stripped pine dresser base with rack added at a later date. $1,045

Oak dresser with split baluster decoration, circa 1860, 59in. wide. $1,070

Victorian mahogany dresser with brass fittings. $1,070

18th century open back oak dresser with scalloped frieze and lower pot shelf, 70in. wide. $1,090

19th century French provincial oak dresser base, 56in. wide, on cabriole legs. $1,140

18th century oak dresser on square legs united by pot board, original iron hooks, 61in. wide. $1,185

Victorian 'Dog Kennel' dresser, circa 1850, 63in. wide. $1,295

Early 19th century stripped pine dresser with pot board. $1,350

An 18th century oak kitchen dresser, 56½in. wide. $1,360

FURNITURE
DRESSERS

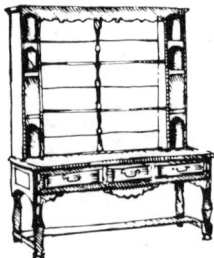

Oak dresser with waved frieze
and open shelves, 65½in. wide.
$1,395

Late 18th century
American pine cup-
board with flat cor-
nice, 48in. wide.
$1,400

An 18th century oak
Welsh dresser with
triple delft rack.
$1,655

George II oak and elm
dresser with three-quar-
ter gallery, circa 1740,
5ft.9½in. wide. $1,730

18th century Lancashire
oak and pine dresser.
$1,800

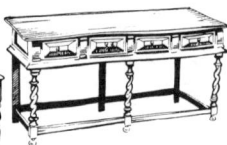

Charles II oak dresser with
brass pear-drop handles,
molded understretchers,
75in. wide. $1,820

George III three drawer oak
dresser with shaped apron,
6ft.11in. wide. $1,820

Charles II oak dresser with
dentil mounted and pierced
cornice, circa 1665, 6ft.3in.
wide. $2,025

Georgian oak dresser with
crossbanded drawers and
split baluster molding,
72in. long. $2,070

18th century French provincial oak buffet, 58¼in. wide. $2,250

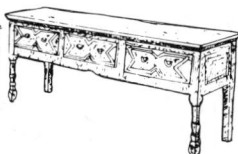

18th century oak dresser with molded rectangular top, 84in. wide. $2,475

18th century oak cross-banded dresser on cabriole legs. $2,735

George II oak and elm dresser with molded cornice, 4ft. 7½in. wide, circa 1750. $2,815

18th century Welsh oak tridarn. $2,880

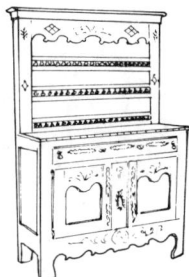

Early 18th century chestnut dresser, known as a buffet-vaisselier, 55in. wide. $3,375

Georgian oak high dresser with divided open shelves and shaped apron, 82in. wide. $3,650

Small Jacobean oak dresser base. $6,075

George II oak dresser with ogee top, circa 1740, 4ft.8½in. wide, later cornice. $8,315

FURNITURE
SHELVES

Victorian stripped pine hanging shelves. $45

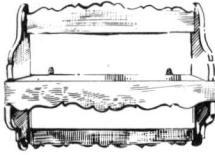

Pinewood kitchen mortar rack to hold two mortars, circa 1780, 23½in. wide. $85

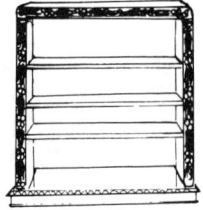

Victorian carved oak open plate rack, 107cm. wide. $110

Stained beech and composition corner bracket, 30in. high, circa 1880. $115

Set of stripped pine hanging bookshelves, George III period, 38in. long. $125

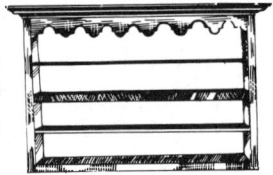

Late 18th century oak two-shelved hanging plate rack. $170

Mahogany Regency set of hanging shelves with carved cresting, circa 1820, 26½in. wide. $215

Victorian carved oak open shelves of three tiers, with spiral supports. $275

19th century mahogany 'Chinese Chippendale' style three-tier wall shelf with fretwork gallery, 56cm. wide. $295

KITCHENWARE

SHELVES

FURNITURE

Dutch triangular hanging shelves with carved top, circa 1820, 31½in. wide. $330

Aesthetic movement mahogany hanging cabinet, signed CWM, dated 1888, 44cm. wide. $370

George III turned mahogany hanging bookshelves, 33in. wide. $395

Yewwood hanging display cabinet of Queen Anne style, 23in. wide. $395

Victorian carved oak serving trolley. $440

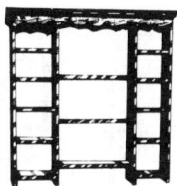

Attractive oak Delft rack, circa 1740, 46in. wide x 45½in. high. $505

One of a pair of mahogany corner shelves, mid 19th century, 34in. high. $630

One of a pair of late 19th century mahogany hanging shelves, 36¼in. wide. $720

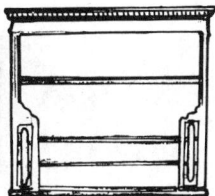

Queen Anne style oak hanging Delft or pewter plate rack, circa 1720. $810

FURNITURE
TABLES

18th century elm cricket table. $100

Late 18th century oak side table on square legs. $110

Elm kneading trough with shaped apron and trestle legs, 3ft.6in. wide. $130

Oak side table with single drawer under, 29in. wide. $175

19th century mahogany washstand on turned legs. $190

Victorian oak gateleg dining table with a carved border and spiral legs. $225

17th century oak center table, 27in. wide. $280

Late 18th century carved oak lowboy, 3ft. wide. $280

18th century mahogany circular tray topped table on tripod base. $315

KITCHENWARE

TABLES

FURNITURE

18th century walnut chateau wine tasting table with folding top. $340

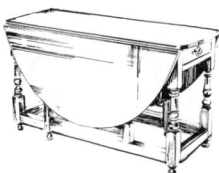

Late 19th century oak gateleg table with oval top. $345

18th century American painted pine water bench, upper shelf with splashback, 26½in. wide. $400

Modern George III style mahogany dumb waiter with two foliate molded tiers, 24in. diam. $405

George III mahogany dropleaf dining table on tapering legs. $445

Late 18th century country Chippendale mahogany tea table, 72cm. wide. $450

Mid 18th century George III elm cricket table, top 25in. diam. $545

Early 19th century Dutch mahogany tea kettle stand with cover or cellarette, 26in. high. $700

Early 19th century Shaker cherry and birch candlestand, Massachusetts, 26¾in. high. $700

FURNITURE
TABLES

Mid 17th century oak gateleg table, 36in. wide. $765

18th century provincial painted table with single gate, 42in. long. $850

Unusual Regency mahogany tray-top table with two galleried tiers, the upper lifting off, 31¼in. wide. $890

Oak coaching table with oval folding top, 3ft.6in. wide, circa 1800. $930

Farmhouse oak refectory table with honey-colored patination, circa 1730, 56in. long x 26½in. wide x 29½in. high. $1,000

Regency mahogany breakfast table with a detachable leaf. $1,015

Gustav Stickley oak dropleaf table, circa 1909, 32in. diam., open. $1,100

Regency mahogany twotier dumb waiter with graduated shelves, 25in. diam. $1,110

Mid 18th century New England country Queen Anne cherry and hickory butterfly table, 40in. wide. $1,200

KITCHENWARE

TABLES

George II bottle rack on walnut stand, circa 1750, 2ft.2in. wide. $1,570

Chippendale pine bird cage candlestand, New England, circa 1780, 14½in. diam. $1,795

Cherrywood inlaid dining table with drop leaves, circa 1790, 48in. wide. $1,800

Late 17th century Welsh farmhouse table with an ash top and oak underframe. $2,880

Early 19th century Shaker cherrywood drop-leaf table, 29in. wide. $3,000

Early 19th century Irish George III style wine tasting table with attachable tray. $3,300

Rare oak refectory table with three-plank top on stepped bases, 8ft.4½in. long. $3,700

Early 18th century William and Mary butterfly table, 38½in. diam. $3,970

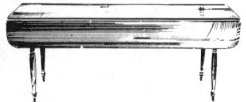

Federal painted harvest table, New England, circa 1810, 72in. long. $4,725

111

GLASS UTENSILS

Victorian octagonal glass ink bottle. $15

Pair of cut glass pickle jars and covers on a plated stand. $36

Victorian glass fly catcher. $72

Glass match striker with silver container, Mappin Bros., 1896. $80

One of a set of seven Victorian glass wine coolers, 14cm. diam. $80

One of a pair of Victorian pear-shaped decanters, 22.5cm. high. $90

Late 18th century candlestick with flat cut stem. $90

Mid 19th century Bristol clear glass wine cooler with characteristic prismatic cutting round the neck. $145

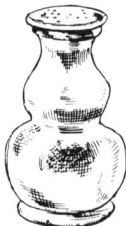

Early 20th century Tiffany gold iridescent pepper shaker, New York, 2¾in. high. $150

GLASS UTENSILS

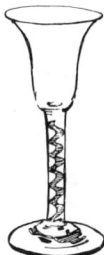

Wine glass with wide bell bowl on a stem with single mercury corkscrew, 7in. high, circa 1750. $155

19th century glass decanter, Bristol red, with plated stopper. $165

Unusual stirrup glass, early 18th century, 6¼in. high. $185

A small Mary Gregory amber glass pin tray depicting a boy with a butterfly net. $190

Molded glass pomade jar in the form of a bear, Sandwich, Massachusetts, circa 1845, 3¾in. high. $200

One of three circular glass candle holders, marked R. Lalique, 14.4cm. diam. $220

Wine glass with ogee bowl, circa 1750, 6¾in. high. $295

Victorian tobacco jar bearing 'The Jolly Japers'. $340

One of a pair of engraved decanters, circa 1760, 9½in. high. $450

113

GLASS UTENSILS

Pair of Victorian glass gilded decanters, circa 1860, 12in. high. $450

Unusual glass candlestick, 8¼in. high, with beaded high domed foot.
$460

Electroplated mounted frosted and cut glass whisky barrel and tot, 1863. $475

A custard glass with round funnel bowl, 18th century, 4¼in. high. $475

Central European milchglas enameled tankard, 5½in. high, circa 1750.
$485

Pressed glass miniature covered tureen, Sandwich, Massachusetts, circa 1828, 3in. long.
$600

Part of a thirty-two-piece Bohemian glass drinking set, late 19th century.$605

Dutch 19th century decanter with silver mounts.
$630

Pair of apothecary jars marked 'Castor Oil Seeds' and 'Cassia', with original contents, 10in. high. $710

Rare glass globular teapot
and cover, circa 1725,
15cm. wide. $770

A gilded blue glass
tulip design wine
cooler signed by
Isaac and Lazarus.
$790

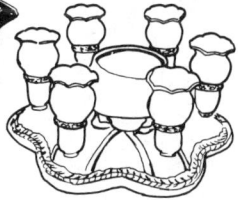

Coffee and cream glass
centerpiece by Webbs,
10¼in. diam. $790

Rectangular two-bottle
decanter stand by Reily
& Storer, London, 1836,
26cm. long, 28.6oz.$980

Two from a set of six
etched and cut glass spirit
bottles, circa 1840.
$1,125

Good Moser glass set, circa
1900, in clear glass with
floral decoration.
$1,240

G. BRANDY

ORANGE BITTERS

Green glass decanter by J.
Giles, 9¼in. high, circa
1775. $1,295

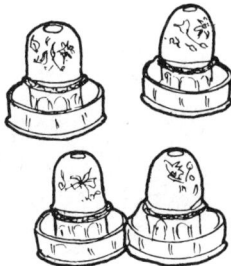

Set of four Burmese fairy
lights. $1,635

Good Loetz iridescent glass
'rosewater sprinkler', 24cm.
high, circa 1900.
$2,410

115

GONGS

Late 19th century oak framed gong. $35

A Victorian brass table gong on an oak base. $65

Late 19th century brass gong with beater on a bamboo stand. $80

Oriental bronze table bell, on carved and pierced ironwood stand. $110

Table gong supported by two carved elephants, 2ft. 11in. wide. $100

Victorian brass gong complete with striker. $135

19th century Oriental gong with carved hardwood stand. $165

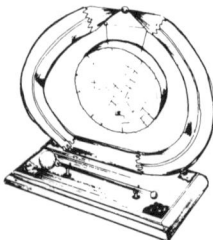

Burmese brass gong supported by carved ivory tusks. $170

Late 19th century bronze bell on hardwood stand, 38in. high. $295

116

KITCHENWARE

GOBLETS

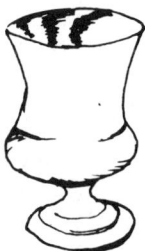

A 19th century yew wood goblet. $30

A walnut goblet on stem. $35

A Scottish carved wood goblet on a stem, 10¼in. high. $70

GRAPE HODS

19th century oak and copper grape hod. $180

An embossed brass grape carrier. $235

18th century German copper grape hod, 1ft.10in. high. $450

GRAPE SCISSORS

Pair of late 19th century vine pattern grape scissors, 18cm. long, 3.8oz. $175

Silver grape scissors by Mappin & Webb, Sheffield 1902. $200

King's pattern silver grape scissors by Mary and Charles Reily, 1826. $225

Pair of William IV silver gilt grape scissors, by William Traies, London, 1833, 4oz.14dwt. $750

KITCHENWARE

GRIDDLES

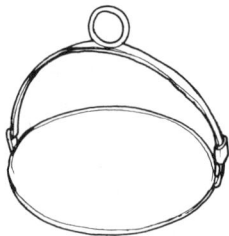

19th century iron griddle. $55

Queen Anne wrought iron gridiron with four feet to stand on embers, circa 1700, 9in. square. $100

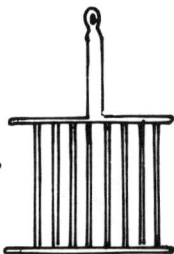

18th century iron steak griddle, circa 1720.$135

HEATERS

Late 19th century brass framed heater on paw feet.$110

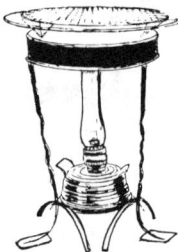

Victorian 'Ardent' brass heating lamp on a wrought iron stand with a copper top. $145

Victorian cast iron Cathedral heater. $190

HONEY POTS

Belleek honey pot, 5in. high. $70

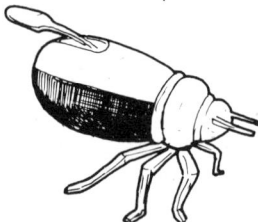

Silver plated honey pot with green glass body. $235

An iridescent glass honey pot.$460

KITCHENWARE

HOOKS

Queen Anne period steel game hook. $55

A saw-type pot hanger of polished steel, circa 1690, 26in. long. $90

Carved wooden native food hook. $285

ICE CREAM EQUIPMENT

Late 19th century ice cream scoop. $5

Late 19th century ice cream mold of tin. $15

Late 19th century ice cream maker. $70

IRON STANDS

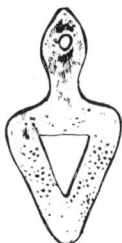

19th century sheet steel flat iron stand with triangular pierced motif, 8½in. long. $20

19th century cast brass flat iron stand with pierced star motif and heavy peg legs, 9¾in. long. $35

Thick brass flat iron stand, circa 1850, 11in. long. $65

IRONS

Victorian flat iron.
$10

Small Victorian
smoothing iron.
$15

William Cross & Sons
'Hot Cross' gas iron.
$25

A large 18lb. goose iron.
$35

Victorian flat iron complete
with pierced iron stand. $45

Victorian box iron.
$45

An early Scottish
box iron. $55

A box iron by Kenrick,
size 6, circa 1870. $55

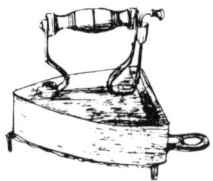

19th century iron
complete with
heating stone and
stand. $55

Petrol heated iron, by
Coleman, model 8
'Instant Lite'. $55

An early Dutch box
iron. $65

An early iron and
brass flat iron. $75

Georgian brass
goffering iron,
circa 1830. $75

18th century brass box iron
and brass trivet. $90

A fine early iron
and brass flat iron.
          $90

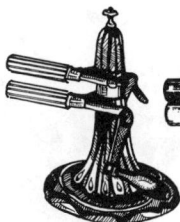

American fluting
iron, circa 1870.
$105

Patent crimping machine.
          $135

An unusual brass
iron of about 1720
with original stone.
$170

JARDINIERES

Royal Doulton art pot about 1902-22, 7½in. wide x 8½in. high. $55

Stylish brass jardiniere about 1900, with three supports and pierced-work band round the body. $70

A 19th century Chinese porcelain jardiniere with blue and white prunus flower decoration, 8in. $80

19th century Satsuma jardiniere decorated with figure scenes, 26cm. diam. $115

19th century Satsuma jardiniere decorated with figure scenes, 27.5cm. high. $135

Late 19th century jardiniere, 14½in. high x 17in. deep. $170

A 19th century Japanese Imari jardiniere, 13in. diam. $225

Regency brass and copper jardiniere with embossed Coat of Arms, 10in. high. $280

Chinese blue and white jardiniere, 1830. $360

Late 19th century Imari jardiniere painted and gilt, 31cm. high. $360

Late 19th century Oriental bronze jardiniere, 53cm. high. $370

One of two Paris jardinieres painted with birds and flowers, 4¾in. diam. $450

De Morgan jardiniere, bell body with twin lug handles, 21.5cm. high. $540

Sevres oval jardiniere of lobed outline, 1759, 9in. wide, painted with flowers. $550

17th century porcelain jardiniere, painted in underglaze blue, 9in. diam. $565

A Canton jardiniere and stand, 22.5cm. high, circa 1880. $600

Massive Liberty & Co. earthenware jardiniere, 76cm. diam., circa 1905. $600

One of a pair of Victorian cast iron Warwick style jardinieres, 77cm. high. $670

JARDINIERES

Late 19th century Imari jardiniere with panels of vases of flowers, 35cm. wide. $705

Doulton stoneware jardiniere and stand, 39¾in. high, circa 1900. $730

Martin Brothers jardiniere with bell body, dated 3-1886, 21.8cm. high. $955

A 19th century Chinese jardiniere, 16in. high and 18in. diam. $980

19th century Chinese rectangular blue and white jardiniere, 13in. $1,070

Late 18th century Wedgwood caneware jardiniere, 6in. long. $1,465

Rookwood sterling overlay standard glaze jardiniere, Ohio, circa 1907, 5½in. high. $1,500

Imari style jardiniere and stand. $2,025

Second Empire bronze jardiniere with circular rim, circa 1860, 61cm. diam. $2,305

124

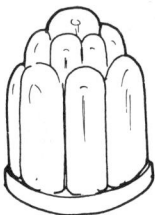

Victorian china
jelly mold. $15

Edwardian glass rabbit
jelly mold. $20

Victorian copper jelly
mold. $55

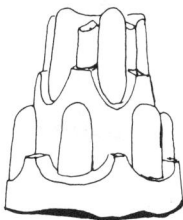

Victorian copper jelly
mold. $65

Copper jelly mold.
$75

19th century copper
jelly mold. $75

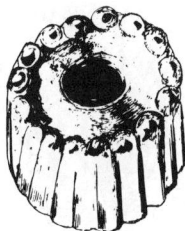

**Large Victorian
copper jelly mold.**
$90

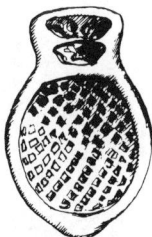

Copeland pineapple
jelly mold, circa
1860. $100

One of a pair of early
19th century pewter
jelly molds by William
Scott, Edinburgh,
circa 1810, 5in. high.
$550

JUGS
CHINA

Victorian black
glazed pottery
water jug. $10

An unmarked
pottery hot
water jug. $20

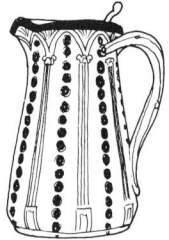

Victorian milk jug
with a pewter lid.
$30

Victorian basin jug
decorated with hand
painted floral designs.
$30

Late 18th century Spode
octagonal shaped jug
with serpent handle, im-
pressed mark, 7¼in. high.
$55

Caughley cream jug in
underglaze blue, circa
1780, 3¼in. high.
$90

Staffordshire saltglaze pear-
shaped milk jug, circa 1755,
8.5cm. high. $135

Glazed earthenware musi-
cal jug, circa 1935, 10in.
high. $205

Liverpool earthenware
lead glaze jug, circa
1700. $215

CHINA   **JUGS**

Bow blue and white cider
jug, circa 1754, 8¼in. high.
$225

18th century German
Peterskirchen stoneware
handled jug with pewter
lid, 18in. high. $250

Early Bow cream jug with
sparrow-beak spout, 3½in.
high, circa 1755. $285

Liverpool creamware
jug, transfer printed
in black, circa 1785.
$305

Royal Worcester jug
with lion's profile,
circa 1880, 9in. high.
$325

Bristol jug decorated
with swags of flowers
in polychrome, 4¾in.
high. $370

Caughley porcelain mask jug
with floral decoration.
$515

18th century German pewter
mounted stoneware flagon
with applied white decoration,
13½in. high. $1,000

Martin Brothers
mask jug, 6¼in.
high. $1,080

JUGS
COPPER & BRASS

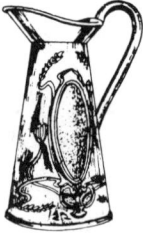

An Art Nouveau copper water jug, 12in. high. $35

Late 19th century copper jug with shaped iron handle, 4½in. high. $40

A copper, Jersey pattern milk jug, 10in. high. $45

American Art Deco copper water jug with spherical body, circa 1930, 12in. high. $45

Victorian copper jug and cover, 18in. high. $45

An Eastern copper and brass jug with domed cover. $45

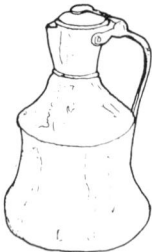

Late 19th century Eastern copper jug and cover. $45

A 19th century copper jug with loop handle and riveted band, 11in. high. $65

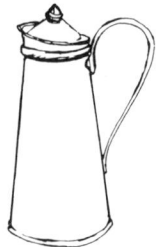

18th century copper hot water jug. $75

KITCHENWARE

A very unusual, shaped, copper spirit jug with tinned interior, circa 1840, 8in. high. $90

Late 18th century copper jug, 11in. high. $100

19th century brass jug with tapered body and dome, hinged cover. $110

Double-lidded copper hot milk container.$220

George III tavern coffee pot in copper, 10in. high. $260

Fine copper wine flagon, brass handle, base and rim, 12½in. high, circa 1710. $280

English brass and copper covered pitcher, circa 1900, 15¼in. high. $340

19th century brass ritual water ewer from Borneo, 11in. long. $370

Swiss cylindrical bell jug, circa 1735.$505

129

JUGS
GLASS

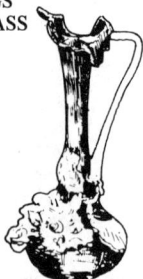

Victorian ruby glass jug
with applied white glass
flowers, 10in. high.
$65

Plated metal and glass
lemonade jug, engraved,
22cm. high, with ebon-
ized wooden handle.
$145

French glass ale jug, circa
1790. $170

Eastern United States cut
glass footed pitcher with
paneled pouring spout,
circa 1880, 9in. high.
$200

Glass water pitcher by
Hawkes, Corning, New
York, circa 1900, 8½in.
high. $200

Lynn glass pear-shaped
cream jug with everted rim
and scroll handle, circa
1770, 9cm. high. $240

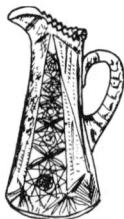

American cut glass cham-
pagne jug, circa 1890,
13½in. high with flared
rim. $300

Cut glass Irish jug with
applied loop handle, circa
1820, 7¾in. high.
$310

Blown three mold glass
jug with wide flaring rim
and pouring spout, circa
1828, 6¼in. high. $425

130

GLASS

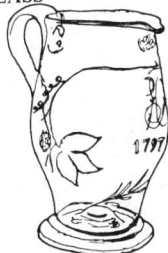

English ale jug, engraved with hops and barley and dated 1797, 7in. high. $450

Late 19th century cameo glass metal mounted jug in cranberry colored glass. $585

Cased wheeling peach blow pitcher, 5½in. high. $650

Silver mounted clear glass claret jug by J. Grinsell & Sons, Ltd., London, 1898, 27.5cm. high. $650

Late 19th century cut glass water pitcher, Eastern United States, 6½in. high, with saw-tooth rim. $700

Early Ravenscroft 'crizzled' decanter jug, circa 1674, 20cm. high. $710

Victorian silver mounted clear glass lotus claret jug, 7¼in. high, by E. H. Stockwell, London, 1880. $730

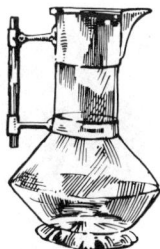

Hukin & Heath Ltd. silver mounted claret jug, London, 1883, 21.5cm. high. $810

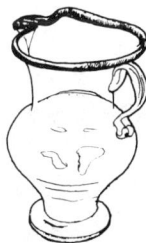

Venetian jug, about 1640, with dark turquoise rim and pinched lip. $1,125

131

KETTLES

**Early 20th century
red enamel kettle
with folding handle
$20**

**Late 19th century
brass kettle. $35**

**Large 19th century seamed
copper kettle with cover,
cast iron handle and brass
tap, 12in. high. $75**

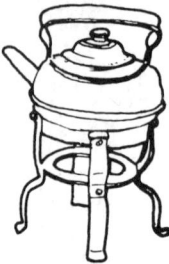

**Small Victorian
copper kettle.$80**

**Victorian circular plated
tea kettle on stand with
hardwood handle, 12in.
high. $85**

**A fine Victorian brass
kettle and stand.$90**

**Brass circular kettle
with amber handle.
$90**

**Victorian plated tea kettle
on lampstand with turned
wood handle, 12in. high.
$95**

**Antique copper kettle with
domed lid and wooden
handle. $100**

132

Victorian copper and brass kettle. $100

Heavy 19th century brass spirit kettle supported by two monkeys, on a stand complete with burner. $110

A copper kettle, the lid with pineapple finial. $110

Unusually large early 19th century square copper kettle. $145

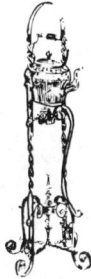

Late Victorian brass spirit kettle on stand, 87cm. high. $145

Very fine three gallon hot water kettle made of cast iron, 18in. high, circa 1840. $145

One of two large copper kettles and covers, 12½in. high. $165

19th century copper and brass kettle with matching stand and burner. $170

Early 19th century American cast iron tilting kettle, 14in. high. $175

133

KETTLES

Brass spirit kettle, with glass handle, circa 1820. $190

Art Nouveau silver plated tea kettle and lampstand. $205

Electroplated teapot, designed by Christopher Dresser, on triangular stand with burner, 19.5cm. high. $215

Benham & Froud copper and brass kettle, designed by Christopher Dresser, 77cm. high. $230

Mid/late Edo period iron tetsubin with rounded sides, signed Ryubundo Zukuri. $225

Superb 18th century copper kettle on stand. $235

Brass electric kettle designed by Peter Behrens, circa 1920, 22.75cm. high. $240

W. Benson copper and brass kettle and burner, 11½in. high, 1890's. $260

Kinkozan earthenware kettle and cover painted and gilt on a blue ground, circa 1900, 13cm. high. $285

Large copper kettle, circa 1760. $305

Earthenware kettle and cover painted with panels of Samurai in gardens, circa 1900, 13cm. high. $325

Large copper Scandinavian coffee kettle, about 1770, 14in. high. $360

George V tea kettle, stand and lamp by Goldsmiths & Silversmiths Co. Ltd., 48oz. $590

Bruder Frank kettle and stand, circa 1900, in silver colored metal. $675

George III tea kettle with stand and burner by R. Crossley, London, 1799, 42oz. $820

Coalbrookdale kettle on stand with flower encrusting. $1,190

Large Russian tea kettle on stand with lobed body, 1887, 15¼in. high, 107oz. $1,450

Large pear-shaped tea kettle, stand and lamp by R. Smith, Dublin, 1843, 15¼in. high, 119oz. $2,900

135

KNIFE BOXES

A mahogany knife box with shaped front, fitted as a stationery case, 14½in. high. $100

George III mahogany knife box. $125

George III mahogany cutlery box inlaid with boxwood lines, 15½in. high. $155

Late 18th century mahogany knifebox. $175

George III mahogany knife box, top with silver crest mount, 34cm. high. $195

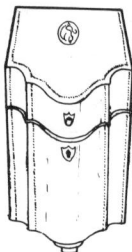

Late 18th century inlaid mahogany knife box with serpentine shaped front. $200

Late 18th century mahogany knife box. $260

Late 18th century mahogany knife box with ornate brass keyhole escutcheon. $395

One of a pair of mahogany knife boxes with rosewood banding and shaped fronts, 12in. high. $400

Mahogany bombe knife box, shell handle and satinwood stringing. $400

George III mahogany knife box with boxwood string inlay fitted with twenty-three knives and forks. $480

George III satinwood cutlery box with serpentine hinged lid, 19cm. wide. $585

One of a pair of 19th century mahogany knife boxes, with shaped fronts, 15¾in. high. $700

One of a pair of Sheraton mahogany inlaid knife boxes with serpentine shaped fronts, 14½in. high. $750

One of a pair of George III mahogany knife boxes with fitted interiors and plated mounts, circa 1780, 9in. wide. $1,105

One of a fine pair of mahogany knife boxes with inlaid conch shells. $1,125

Pair of George III mahogany knife boxes, 15in. high. $1,150

One of a pair of George III mahogany knife boxes with sloping tops and silver lock plates, 10in. wide. $1,200

KNIFE BOXES

Georgian mahogany knife box with brass fittings. $1,210

One of a pair of George III mahogany knife boxes, circa 1780, 8¾in. high. $1,240

One of a pair of George III mahogany and in-laid cutlery boxes, 12in. high. $1,270

One of a pair of George III mahogany and fruit-wood banded knife boxes. $1,350

A pair of mid Georgian mahogany cutlery boxes with brass handles, 9¾in. wide. $1,350

One of a pair of Sheraton mahogany inlaid knife boxes with serpentine shaped fronts, the covers with marquetry inlaid oval panels, 14½in. high. $1,500

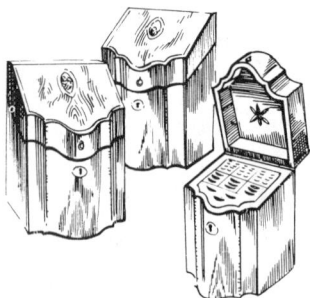

Set of three late 18th century George III knive boxes in mahogany, with inlaid lids. $1,550.

Pair of Georgian mahogany knife boxes. $1,585

Fine set of four 19th century knife boxes. $1,710

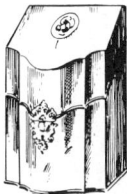

One of a pair of Hepple-white inlaid mahogany knife boxes with brass lock plates, 15in. high. $1,750

A pair of Sheraton knife boxes in mahogany. $2,000

One of a pair of George III satinwood cutlery boxes, 1ft.3in. high, circa 1785. $2,050

One of a pair of George III mahogany and satin-wood knife boxes, 22.5cm. wide. $2,475

An exceptionally fine chinoiserie knife case. $3,600

One of a pair of George III silver mounted mahogany cutlery boxes, 14½in. high, circa 1770. $9,565

LABELS

George III wine label for Port, by John Whittingham, London, 1792. $65

George IV pierced 'Hollands' wine label, by A. W., Edinburgh. $70

George III wine label for Brandy, by Wm. Snooke Hall, 1817. $105

George II wine label for 'Cyder', maker's mark H.P., circa 1758. $215

Pair of George III plain crescent shape wine labels, circa 1790. $195

George III Scottish 'Currant Wine' label by Wm. Parkins, Edinburgh, 1816, 3in. wide. $250

One of two cast wine labels in the mid 18th century style. $295

One of two George III crescent-shaped wine labels, by Hester Bateman, London, 1786-90. $295

George III crescent-shaped wine label, by Hester Bateman, London, 1786-90. $395

Set of silver sauce labels, circa 1800-1825. $710

George III 'Madeira' wine label, by R.S., circa 1783. $1,485

140

A silver mustard ladle by George Adams, London 1850. $15

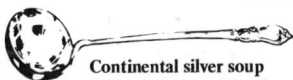

Continental silver soup ladle with chased handle 3oz. $25

Continental silver punch ladle, engraved with chased handle. $45

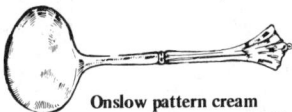

Onslow pattern cream ladle by F. Higgins, 1899. $65

18th century lead pourer, 20½in. long. $80

19th century silver ladle. $125

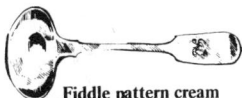

Fiddle pattern cream ladle by J. Bell of Newcastle, 1829. $125

Unmarked Regency punch ladle with turned rosewood handle, 9½in. long. $125

American sterling silver soup ladle with heavily chased handle, 7oz. $200

Silver soup ladle by Hester Bateman, 1782. $360

Fluted silver punch ladle by E. Aldridge, 1742. $360

Silver soup ladle, by Hester Bateman, 1782. $430

Large punch ladle by Wood & Hughes, New York, circa 1870, 15¾in. long, 8 troy oz. $475

Early George II punch ladle by Richard Richardson, Chester, 1733, with turned wood handle. $1,000

141

LAMPS

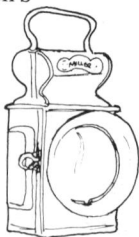

Miller & Co. brass lamp, 9in. high. $45

19th century tin 'bull's eye' lamp. $65

Late 18th century brass oil lamp. $75

A rare tinned sheet iron double crusie or Betty lamp, with pierced flower discs, circa 1850, 12in. high. $75

Brass 'student's' candlestick on square base. $85

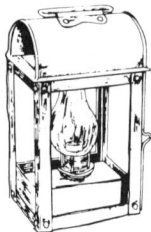

A brass oil lamp with domed top and glazed front and sides, 12½in. high. $90

A brass table oil lamp with a flower painted globe, 1ft.6in. high. $100

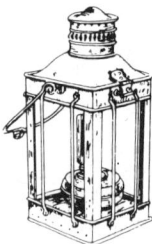

A square copper oil lamp, with chimney and glazed sides with bars, 1ft.3in. high. $110

Victorian brass railway style candle bracket lamp with chimney and coronet. $125

An adjustable, brass, desk oil lamp with white shade. $125

A rare 19th century cast iron wick lamp with detachable screw off lid and swing carrying handle, 11in. high. $125

Miniature American porcelain lamp with globe-shaped opalescent white shade, circa 1880, 9¼in. high. $125

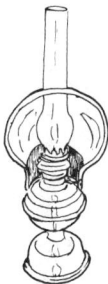

Victorian brass lace maker's lamp with reflector and chimney. $125

Early 20th century Ridsdale brass and copper ship's lantern, 1ft.9in. high. $125

A brass oil lamp with baluster stem, white molded reservoir and shade. $135

A high domed and pierced brass hall lamp, with single suspension handle, 11in. high, circa 1840. $135

One of a pair of adjustable brass railway table/wall lamps with original shades. $140

A brass oil lamp, the reservoir and frosted globe raised on a Corinthian column and molded base, 2ft.5in. high. $145

143

LAMPS

Large Victorian copper street lamp. $145

Edwardian brass desk lamp. $145

Mid 19th century Bulpitt & Sons brass lantern with cylindrical funnel and swing handle, 20in. high. $150

Miniature American cranberry thumb-print lamp with half shade, circa 1880, 7½in. high. $160

Large Victorian oil lamp with pink column and 9in. etched shade. $170

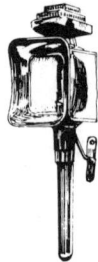

19th century brass carriage lamp. $170

Victorian brass table lamp. $170

Victorian brass oil lamp with cranberry glass bowl and shade, 2ft.3in. high. $170

Victorian brass argand lamp with white glass shades. $175

American half shade table lamp by Bradley & Hubbard, circa 1870, 20in. high. $180

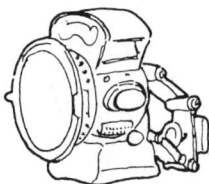

Miller & Co. brass edlite lamp with green and red glass 'bull's eyes' at the sides, the whole on a bicycle mounting, 13cm. high. $180

19th century Italian brass lucerna with four wick spouts, 21¼in. $180

China vase-shaped oil lamp with brass fittings. $190

Ship's masthead riding light in copper, 55cm. high. $190

Lacemaker's lamp with loop handle and pad foot, 23.5cm. high. $205

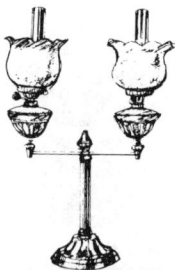

A Victorian brass oil lamp with blue etched globes. $205

Miniature mauve satin glass lamp with half shade, circa 1880, 7in. high. $225

An adjustable oil lamp, with twin burners and green shades. $235

LAMPS

19th century alabaster and brass column table lamp. $235

Miniature American satin glass 'Gone with the Wind' lamp, circa 1880, 8½in. high. $250

Brass and copper lamp, about 1905. $260

A 19th century cut glass oil lamp, on circular base, with shade. $260

Queen Anne brass and horn lantern. $280

Late 18th century brass taper jack, 5½in. high. $290

One of a pair of brass and japanned metal coach lamps by Perry & Turner Ltd., Bristol. $290

A very handsome Victorian oil lamp made in bronze and Paris porcelain, circa 1860. $295

Miniature American cranberry glass lamp with molded dot and panel shade and font, circa 1880, 9½in. high. $325

146

Modernist lamp with spherical green glass shade on blue glass base, 1930's, 31cm. high. $360

Taperstick by Christian Hammer in the form of a sandalled foot, Stockholm, 1857, 5¼in. long. $360

One of a pair of French ormolu table electric lamps with bronze child stems, seated on gilt metal tortoises, 13in. high. $405

Victorian opaline and ormolu lamp for oil, circa 1870, 2ft.7in. high. $450

Small Queen Anne pierced and engraved wall sconce, about 1714, 6½in. high. $485

Fulper pottery lamp, Flemington, New Jersey, circa 1900-10. $550

Early 19th century American painted tin and glass whale oil hand lamp, 10¼in. high. $625

Table oil lamp by Hawksworth, Eyre & Co., Sheffield, 1912. $790

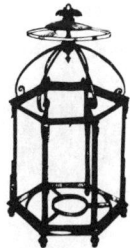

George III bronze framed porch lantern. $1,465

147

KITCHENWARE

LETTER BOXES

A coaching tavern post box of japanned toleware, divided into three compartments, 13in. long, 5in. deep, 6½in. high. $80

Carved oak letter box, circa 1860. $120

Interesting Victorian oak letter box with brass fittings. $170

A country house Royal Mail letter box in pinewood, simulated to appear as mahogany, original black and gilt word 'Letters', 24½in. high. $395

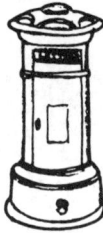

Oak country house letter box formed as a miniature pillar box, 16in. high. $475

Victorian oak pillar letter box, 24in. high. $900

LETTER RACKS

19th century brass letter clip by Merry, Phipson & Parker. $25

Victorian brass letter rack. $45

Victorian papier mache letter rack. $90

KITCHENWARE

LIQUEUR & WATER SETS

A modernist cocktail service, consisting of a decanter and six glasses, circa 1930. $225

Modernist glass liqueur set with tray, 1930's. $305

Suite of table glass by R. Lalique, France, thirty-five pieces in all. $330

Unusual gilt water set of eight pieces, circa 1900, jug 30.5cm. high. $420

Etched liqueur service in glass, 1930's. $495

Clear and amber stained glass carafe and stopper with six glasses en suite, inscribed R. Lalique, France. $740

Part of a late 19th century Stourbridge glass table service of fifty-two pieces. $800

Part of a one hundred and twenty-eight-piece gilt glass table service, circa 1900. $830

Etched enameled and applied glass ewer and glasses by E. Galle, signed. $1,850

149

LOG CONTAINERS

A brass bound copper
log pail with swing
handle. $70

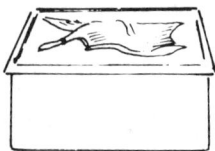

Victorian oak log
box with embossed
copper lid, 79cm.
wide. $125

Art Nouveau style brass and
iron log container.$120

Circular copper
log cauldron with
brass handles and
claw feet. $125

19th century copper log
pail with swing handle.
      $180

Large early 19th century
copper log container with
lion mask handles and paw
feet. $185

18th century Dutch
brass log cauldron
on paw feet. $260

Early 19th century
pierced brass log
box with liner,
13in. high. $280

Fine 19th century brass log
container with embossed
decoration. $645

KITCHENWARE

MATCH CASES

Match case commemorating the Silver Jubilee of George V and Queen Mary. $35

Angel match box holder, Birmingham, 1903. $35

Silver match case with fluted decoration. $55

Silver match case with floral decoration. $80

Metal match case in the form of a Gladstone bag. $115

Vesta match case showing Edward VII, 1901. $170

Victorian silver vesta box with embossed horse race scene. $170

French Art Nouveau silver smoker's set, circa 1900. $270

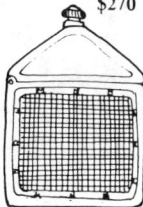

Vesta match case advertising Otto Monsteds Margarines. $295

Enameled silver vesta case, Birmingham, 1888. $280

Silver vesta case, 1913. $305

Golfer match box by Sampson Morden & Co., 1891. $530

MEASURES

Tinned iron whisky dipping measure. $20

George III copper measure. $65

A 19th century copper gallon spirit measure. $75

Late 19th century thistle measure with Glasgow tree. $75

Large 19th century lidded Scottish measure. $90

19th century copper measure with loop handle, 10in. high. $95

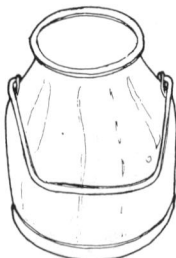

Copper and brass five gallon measure with iron handle. $110

A set of three Victorian copper measures with iron handles and brass plate engraved 'Cider'. $125

Antique pewter belly measure, circa 1820, stamped 'Pint', 5¼in. high. $125

Early 19th century two-gallon copper measure of circular form, 15in. high. $135

Bushel corn measure, iron banded, circa 1840. $135

Early 19th century four-gallon copper and brass measure inscribed R. Cain. $146

One gallon copper spirit measure, dovetail seams, circa 1850. $175

Steel banded wooden corn measure, stamped KP, circa 1790, 16½in. diam., 14in. high. $215

A copper four gallon measure. $215

Early 18th century lidded baluster measure of half-pint capacity, 4¼in. high. $260

Set of William IV grain measures in wood. $270

Brass standard measure. $270

MEASURES

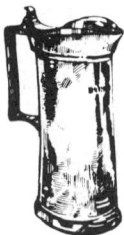

French 19th century pewter, lidded, double litre measure, 10in. $325

Early 19th century one gallon harvest measure with scroll handle, 11½in. high. $415

French lidded cylindrical measure, 19th century, 11in. high. $530

Early 18th century pewter 'ball' measure of conventional form, by Edward Quick, 9cm. high. $540

19th century South African Imperial gallon standard bronze measure with ebony handles, 20cm. diam. $560

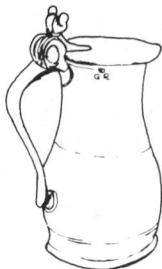

Jersey pewter wine measure of typical form, about 5½in. high. $620

Late 17th/early 18th century pewter 'ball' measure of half pint capacity, 12.5cm. high. $675

Unusual set of three copper and brass spirit measures, circa 1850, one gallon, 10½in. high, three gallons, 16in. high, five gallons, 19in. high. $685

Standard bronze measure with container, 1601. $730

154

Scottish pewter tappit hen measure, circa 1800, 11in. high overall. $800

Late 17th/early 18th century pewter 'ball' measure of gill capacity, engraved with initials, 10cm. high. $810

French pewter pitchet or wine measure, circa 1735-50. $880

Guernsey, lidded pot measure in pewter, mid 18th century, by A. Carter, 11¼in. high. $990

Bud baluster measure of half pint capacity, by John Carr, touch dated 1697, 5¼in. tall. $990

Late 17th century rare 'hammer-head' baluster measure in pewter, half pint capacity, 12cm. high. $1,015

A Scots baluster measure of quart capacity by William Scott of Edinburgh, 20cm. high, circa 1800. $1,155

Irish gallon 'haystack' measure in pewter, circa 1860, 12in. high overall. $1,265

Rare late 17th/early 18th century pewter 'ball' measure of one pint capacity, 17.5cm. high. $1,395

MEASURES

Early 18th century North Country pewter baluster measure with flat cover, 6½in. high. $1,425

One of a set of seven Leeds brass bound copper conical measures, inscribed City of Leeds, in fitted pine case. $1,430

A rare Irish gallon haystack measure by William Seymour, 29.5cm. high, circa 1825. $1,485

One of a set of three Dewsbury brass conical measures, by D. Grave & Co., London, 1893. $1,545

17th century pewter 'wedge' baluster measure of quart capacity, 21.5cm. high. $1,575

18th century English pewter gallon baluster measure with shaped handle, 32cm. high. $1,800

Set of seven pewter haystack measures, 3in. to 11½in. high. $1,980

One of a set of eight Huddersfield brass conical measures by D. Grave & Co., London.
$2,360

Baluster shaped wine measure of gallon capacity by Thomas Stevens of London, 33.2cm. high, circa 1735. $2,640

A gallon size bud measure with maker's mark E.S., 12¾in. high, circa 1680.
$2,970

Set of six copper brass bound checkpump petroleum measures from 5 gallons to ½ gallon. $3,190

One of a set of eleven brass conical measures, inscribed Corpn. of Halifax, 1893.
$3,215

Set of ten gun-metal standard capacity measures from bushel to quarter gill. $3,940

One of a set of twelve cylindrical brass measures, from 5 gallons to ¼ gill.
$4,730

157

MILKING EQUIPMENT

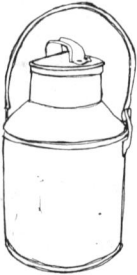

Small Victorian brass milk churn. $35

Milkman's copper cream dipper, 22½in. long, 4in. cup. $45

A milkman's quart tin milk dipper with a curved brass handle to hang on the edge of the churn, circa 1850, 4in. high excluding handle. $55

Victorian copper milk pail with brass handles. $75

18th century Dutch brass milk churn. $180

Dutch copper milk pail with snap-over cover, 16in. high. $200

Dairy shop's pottery milk bucket, named 'Pure Milk', 12in. high, circa 1850. $235

Milkmaid's copper bucket with swing over handle, circa 1820. $270

One of a pair of mid 19th century English brass milk churns, 17in. high. $1,380

MILK JUGS

George III milk jug, London, 1812, with reeded handle. $185

Meissen chinoiserie hot milk jug and cover painted by C. F. Herold, circa 1725, 15cm. high. $830

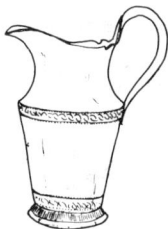

Swiss milk jug, 7¾in. high, Lausanne, 1800, 12oz.16dwt. $900

MORTARS

George I English bronze mortar, 3½in. high, circa 1720. $85

English bronze mortar and pestle, circa 1690. $340

Early 17th century English bronze mortar, 6in. high, and a pestle 8¼in. long. $450

MOLDS

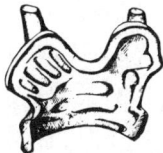

One of a pair of red pottery sweetmeat molds in the form of chickens, circa 1850, 4½in. long. $50

Copper and tin pork pie mold, circa 1880. $70

A late 19th century copper mold. $80

159

MUGS

Cylindrical mug by Atkin Brothers, Sheffield, 1887, 5.3oz., 9.8cm. high. $125

Pewter pint mug with reeded band and base stamped WR., 15½cm. high. $130

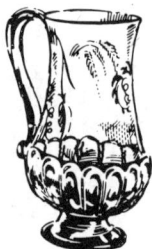

Engraved coin ale mug of bell shape, 6¾in. high. $250

Bow mug of cylindrical shape with slightly flared base, circa 1755-60, 5¾in. high. $275

Small Worcester mug of cylindrical shape with loop handle, 2¼in. high circa 1760-65. $345

Staffordshire pearlware commemorative mug, 4¼in. high. $350

Delft mug, about 1750, English or Dutch, 7¼in. high. $405

Rare Caughley mug printed in underglaze blue, 3¼in. high. $1,285

A fine mid 18th century Worcester commemorative mug. $1,855

Rectangular mustard pot with fluted decoration by Finley & Taylor, London, 1883, 2.9oz. $105

Tapering cylindrical mustard pot and spoon by Robert Hennell, London, 1848-51, 6.4oz. $185

Italian mustard pot and stand, Naples, 1792, stand 4½in. diam., 7oz.10dwt. $385

George III vase-shaped mustard pot, 5in. high, by Robt. Hennell I, London, 1790, and spoon, 5oz. 1dwt. $565

Mustard pot and caster en suite, late 18th century, 6¼in. high, 11oz. 12dwt. $565

Silver gilt mustard pot and spoon, London and Birmingham, 1838, 5.2oz. $890

Unusual early Victorian mustard pot by Richard Sibley, London, 1841, 4¾in. diam., 12oz. $915

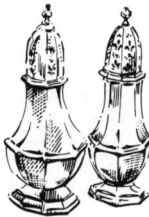

George I octagonal caster and dry mustard pot, 4½in. high, London, 1722, 5oz.13dwt. $2,475

Silver gilt mustard pot by John Bridge, 1825, 24oz. $5,535

KITCHENWARE

NECESSAIRES

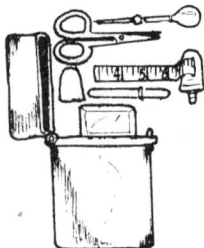

Lady's sewing case in brilliant blue papier mache, circa 1840, 3¾in. high. $260

Early Victorian, European leather necessaire with an ivory plaque depicting a romanticized rural domestic scene. $260

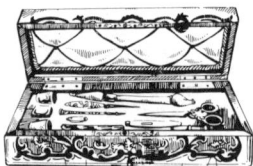

Rectangular necessaire, wood body veneered in mother-of-pearl, 1854, fully fitted. $490

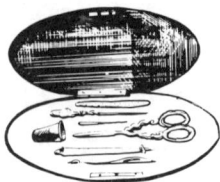

French oval tortoiseshell necessaire with gilt metal inlay, circa 1860, 12.2cm. long. $585

Mother-of-pearl and gilt metal necessaire as a musical box. $700

Antique English brass inlaid rosewood necessaire de voyage, 14in. wide. $750

Early 19th century French musical necessaire, 7.5cm. wide. $1,090

French gold and scarlet lacquer necessaire by Dion, 1771. $1,295

French Empire ormolu and mother-of-pearl necessaire casket, with musical box. $1,395

KITCHENWARE

NIGHT LIGHTS

Victorian green
glass night light.
$15

Staffordshire porcelain
pastille burner cottage,
circa 1840. $190

A night light holder
bearing various scenes.
$280

NUTCRACKERS

'Gladstone' carved
wood nutcrackers,
8in. high, in satin-
wood. $25

Early 18th century Queen
Anne steel nutcrackers,
4½in. long, circa 1710.
$30

A carved wood nutcracker
in the form of a grotesque
man's head, the jaws crack-
ing the nut, circa 1840.
$65

Pair of 19th century walnut
nutcrackers. $370

Victorian silver nutcrac-
kers by Edward Edwards,
1841. $640

Pair of Elizabethan box-
wood nutcrackers, 1583,
4½in. high. $810

NUTMEG GRATERS

Enamel egg-shaped nutmeg grater in yellow and white. $110

George III silver nutmeg grater by Mary Hyde and John Reily, London, 1799, 2in. diam. $225

Silver screw-top egg-shaped grater, maker KS, circa 1800. $225

Rare Sheffield plated cylindrical nutmeg grater case with grater inside, about 1790. $225

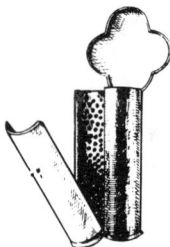

Silver nutmeg grater by Elkington & Co., Birmingham, 1906, 3in. long. $340

Box-type nutmeg grater by William Elliott, 1825. $440

Late 18th century egg-shaped nutmeg grater by Samuel Meriton. $450

Silver nutmeg grater by Rawlings & Sumner, 1842. $495

George III oval nutmeg grater by Roger Biggs, London, 1795, 2in. wide. $495

KITCHENWARE

NUTMEG GRATERS

Staffordshire oviform nutmeg grater, 2¼in. high, circa 1770. $500

Georgian silver nutmeg grater by Phipps & Robinson, London, 1788, 2¾in. high. $565

Vase-shaped nutmeg grater, unmarked, circa 1800, 3½in. high. $575

William IV tube nutmeg grater by Rawlings & Sumner, London, 1835, 2½in. long. $635

George III oval nutmeg grater by Phipps & Robinson, London, 1786, 2¼in. wide. $650

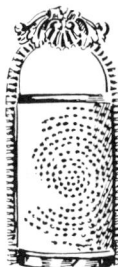

George III oblong hanging nutmeg grater by J. Reily, London, 1818, 4in. long. $655

Unusual clam-shaped nutmeg grater by Hilliard & Thomason, Birmingham, 1853, 4.7cm. wide. $745

Nutmeg grater by W. J., Aberdeen, circa 1830, 1½in. wide. $810

Silver gilt nutmeg grater by John Reily, London, 1793. $850

KITCHENWARE

PADLOCKS

Early 19th century French padlock with oak leaf decoration on key escutcheon cover. $35

17th century bar padlock and key. $100

17th century Germanic or Central European padlock. $235

PAILS

Victorian floral toilet pail with a wicker handle. $55

Victorian brass cider pail. $65

One of a set of four Georgian oyster pails in brass bound mahogany, 10in. diameter.$4,950

PASTRY TRIMMERS

Brass pie trimmer and wheel, circa 1830. $25

Antique brass pastry marker and crimper, circa 1820, 4in. long. $40

Brass pastry jigger and pricker, late 18th century, 4in. long. $45

KITCHENWARE

PEPPERS

Dutch pepper caster in the form of a quail, Chester, 1917, 3¾in. high. $290

William IV bell-shaped pepperette by Charles Fox, London, 1832, 2oz.8dwt., 3in. high. $295

George I cylindrical kitchen pepper by John Hamilton, Dublin, 2½in. high, 2oz.9dwt. $820

PIN BOXES

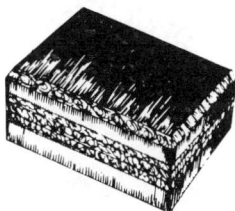

19th century Tunbridgeware pin box. $45

19th century tortoiseshell pin case with a 'Renaissance' miniature on either side. $160

Tortoiseshell and silver pique box, Queen Anne. $280

PLATE WARMERS

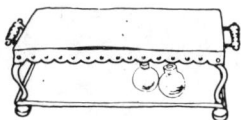

Edwardian double handled copper plate warmer. $64

18th century plate warmer. $215

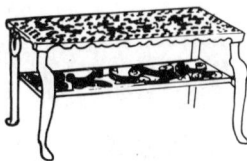

Late 18th century plate warmer in brass and wrought iron, 24in. long. $720

PLATES

Late 18th century Leeds oval creamware plate, 9in. diam. $60

18th century Dutch Delft plate with blue rim, 9in. diam. $100

Early Fulham period De Morgan copper lustre small plate, 6¾in. diam. $710

Bristol delft plate, 9in. diam., about 1750-70. $225

Whieldon pottery plate with raised spotted shaped border, circa 1760. $225

One of a set of eight Royal Worcester plates, 1918, 10½in. diam. $485

One of a rare pair of Derby plates, early 19th century, 8¾in. diam. $1,635

One of twelve late Meissen scale-green ground dinner plates, 10½in. diam. $2,140

Bristol delft powdered manganese plate in underglaze blue. $2,700

Mahogany plate bucket with brass carrying handle. $315

Late 18th century brass bound mahogany plate bucket. $640

Butler's brass bound mahogany plate bucket with a tapered handle and original brasses, circa 1745. $710

A brass handled and banded mahogany plate pail, circa 1755. $720

George III mahogany brass bound plate bucket with swing over brass handle, 37cm. high. $925

George III mahogany and brass bound plate bucket, 12¼in. high. $1,080

One of a pair of George III mahogany plate buckets with brass bands, 14in. diam. $1,505

George III mahogany plate bucket with brass handle and rim, circa 1780, 33cm. high. $1,555

George III mahogany plate pail with brass handle. $2,760

169

KITCHENWARE

POT LIDS

Peace. $90

Small pot lid 'Bears at School', with base.
$110

'Shooting Bears' a small pot lid in good condition, with base.   `$110

Small lid with well-defined print of Bear, Lion and Cock, with base.
$120

Landing the Fare, Pegwell Bay. $125

Large pot lid showing the Exhibitions Buildings, 1851.
$165

'The Trysting Place' a small lid with plain margin. $185

Summer. $215

'Bear Hunting' a small pot lid with retailer's inscription and gilt line border.
$325

Sea Nymph. $360

Extra small pot lid 'Volunteers', framed, in good condition. $380

A False Move, an unusual large pot lid in good condition. $390

KITCHENWARE

Extra small pot lid 'Old Jack', framed. $475

Rare lid 'Strathfield Say', framed, in good condition. $500

Napoleon III with the Empress Eugenie. $630

Rare medium pot lid 'The Tower of London', in good condition. $635

The Garden Terrace, a medium-small lid with raised floral and beehive border. $635

Rare pot lid with a narrow foliate border, maker Robert Feast. $640

Royal Coat of Arms. $710

Pegwell Bay, for S. Banger, Shrimp Sauce Manufacturer, rare large pot lid with clear print. $1,415

Rare large lid with a clear print of Belle Vue Tavern (with Tatnell's cart). $1,510

Pot lid Pet Rabbits. $2,160

Pot lid commemorating the New York Exhibition of 1853. $3,600

Pot lid by Mayer Bros., circa 1850, 12.7cm. diam. $6,480

171

KITCHENWARE

PRESERVING PANS

Victorian brass preserving pan with a folding iron handle. $35

A fine brass preserve pan with swing over carrying handle, circa 1830, 9in. diameter. $90

Early 19th century copper preserving pan. $125

Brass preserving pan with bronze handles, circa 1830, 12½in. diam. $130

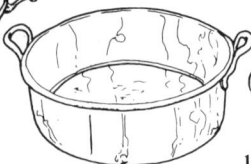

Copper circular double handled pan, 19½in. $155

19th century copper preserve pan with two handles, circa 1840, 13¾in. diam. $190

PUMPS

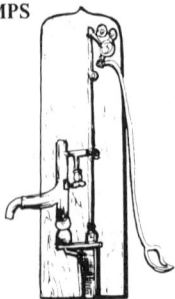

Highly polished brass, steel and lead farmhouse kitchen water pump. $295

Polished steel, bronze and brass water pump, in working order, circa 1800. $305

Small hand pump which belonged to the Birmingham Fire Office. $1,070

KITCHENWARE

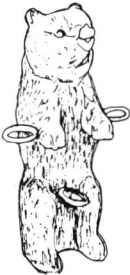

19th century carved bear pipe rack, 11in. tall. $65

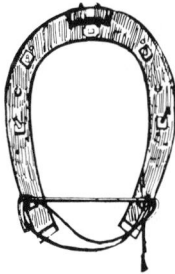

Polished oak and brass huntsman's whip rack, circa 1870. $220

Early 19th century masonic spoonrack in fruitwood, 23in. high. $310

REEL STANDS

19th century treen two-tier reel stand on three bun feet, in mahogany. $145

Regency period ormolu reel stand with the original reels. $170

19th century lignum vitae reel stand. $1,470

ROLLING PINS

Victorian rolling pin. $15

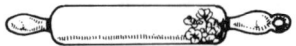

Early 20th century decorated china rolling pin. $35

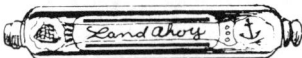

Victorian glass rolling pin. $75

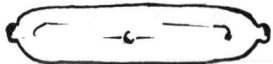

Bristol blue glass sailor's love token. $105

173

RUSHLIGHT HOLDERS

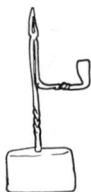

A wrought iron rushlight and candleholder on a wooden base, 17th century. $175

Early 18th century iron hanging rushlight and candleholder, 4ft. long, extending to 6ft. $250

17th century rushlight and candlestand. $250

Queen Anne rushlight holder, 36in. high. $350

A Queen Anne iron rushlight holder, 48in. high, circa 1710. $375

Adjustable Queen Anne wrought iron rushlight and candle stand, circa 1705. $450

18th century English yew-wood rushlight nip, 11½in. high. $680

18th century American oak screw post lighting device, 47in. high. $700

One of a pair of late 17th century iron candleholders. $935

KITCHENWARE

SALAD SERVERS

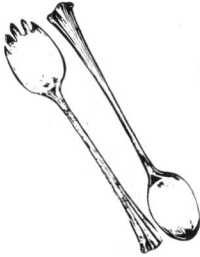

Pair of plated salad servers
made in 1920's. $20

Pair of Victorian plated
servers in case. $30

George III fiddle pattern
salade tongs by Ward S.
Kingdom, London, 1813,
4oz.5dwt. $170

SALAD BOWLS

Victorian china salad
bowl complete with
servers. $65

Victorian turned wood salad
bowl with servers. $65

Circular Doulton Lambeth
salad bowl having blue and
fawn decorations with plated
rim and matching plated servers. $215

SALTS[i]

One of two George III oval
salt cellar stands by Wm.
Abdy, London; 1802, 4oz.
17dwt., 4¾in. wide.
$275

Worcester blue and white shell
salt, circa 1770, 20.5cm. wide.
$570

One of a pair of pedestal
salt cellars with coiled dolphin stems, by Smith
Nicholson & Co., London,
1852. $790

SAMOVARS

A copper circular vase-shaped tea urn with brass handles and spout, 13½in. high. $125

19th century copper samovar. $135

Victorian plated on copper samovar complete with burner. $145

A George III brass globular tea urn, on four legs and ball feet. $170

Early 19th century copper samovar with lion's head drop ring handles and a brass tap. $190

19th century globe-shaped copper tea urn. $230

19th century copper samovar with ebony handles. $265

Large brass samovar and six fitted brass tea glass holders and tray, circa 1900, by V. S. Batacheva, 53.2cm. high. $450

Good 19th century copper samovar, 45cm. high. $440

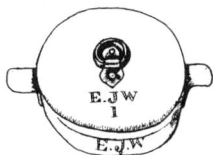

Four various copper lids.
$35

Georgian brass saucepan.
$35

Victorian circular copper picnic saucepan with lid initialed, 5in. diam.$80

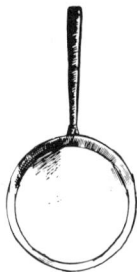

George III copper saucepan with wrought steel handle riveted to pan, 9in. diameter. $100

An early Victorian copper pan with a wooden handle.
$125

Copper frying pan, circa 1780.$135

A good quality bronze skillet on three feet.$125

17th century bell metal skillet. $235

17th century brass and wrought iron skillet on three feet, 23½in. wide.$570

SCALES

Late 19th century brass faced Salter spring balance, up to 41lbs. $55

Polished steel yard sack scales, complete with pear-shaped weight, circa 1790, 25in. long. $80

Pair of 19th century French brass and iron shop scales. $80

Fine pair of Victorian brass letter scales complete with weights. $85

Unusual brass spring balance, circa 1870, weighs up to 12lbs. $85

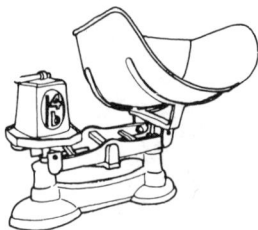

Late Victorian, grocer's scales. $115

Late 19th century American double pan scales with knife blade balance, 75cm. high. $240

Bell metal and brass beam, inscribed Morley, by W. & T. Avery Ltd., Birmingham. $335

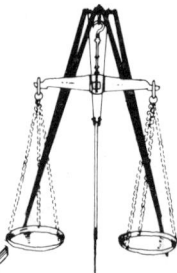

Wakefield 56lb. bell-shaped beam scale measure in fitted mahogany case. $595

KITCHENWARE

Silver cream scoop with rat-tail and wood handle. $55

Silver butter or cheese scoop with mother-of-pearl handle, 1842. $60

Marrow scoop, Samuel Pemberton, Birmingham, 1802. $115

Marrow scoop by Samuel Godbehere. $170

Silver marrow scoop by E.B., London, 1745. $250

Combined silver marrow scoop and table spoon by Elias Cachart, 1750. $395

CRUMB

Late 19th century brass crumb tray. $5

Late Victorian brass crumb scoop. $15

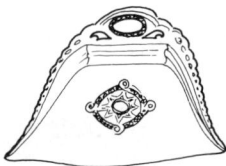

Victorian brass crumb scoop. $20

Art Nouveau brass crumb scoop. $30

Victorian silver crumb scoop with ivory handle. $65

Lacquer crumb tray and brush painted with chinoiserie scenes. $70

SEWING ITEMS

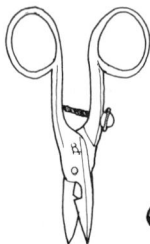

Steel buttonhole scissors, made in Sheffield by Walker & Hall, about 1920. $5

Early wooden knitting sheath in elm. $20

Victorian silver thimble in a mother-of-pearl case. $20

Victorian ivory sewing reel. $20

19th century wooden needle case and thread spool. $20

Brass 'Hemming Bird' surmounted by a pin-cushion. $100

Silver pin cushion in the form of a chick, Chester, 1906. $100

20th century sterling silver and enamel thimble case of egg shape, 4cm. high. $185

Chelsea thimble in hinged silver filigree case, circa 1700, 2cm. high. $2,880

SEWING MACHINES

Wanzer lock-stitch sewing machine on marble base.   **$55**

Small French sewing machine, 8in. high.   **$125**

An English arm-and-platform sewing machine, dated 1877. $250

Sewing machine by Wheeler & Wilson, circa 1854.   **$580**

Britannia Wheeler & Wilson lock-stitch type sewing machine with cast iron treadle table. $1,220

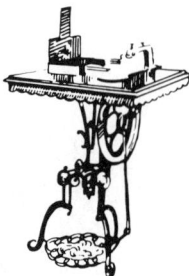

Late 19th century Wheeler & Wilson type Britannia sewing machine.   **$1,495**

SIGNS

Tin advertisement for Pearson's Antiseptic. $35

Enameled sign of an elf in red costume, 30 x 24in. $180

Shaped, printed and enameled sign for Depot for Oceanic Footwear, 13 x 19in. $190

Sunlight Soap, enamel sign of boy holding bars of Sunlight soap, 33½ x 32½in., circa 1905. $320

'Selo Film' enamel sign in yellow, red and black, 14in. wide. $355

Enameled sign advertising Robin Starch, 35½ x 29½in. $360

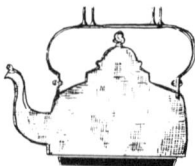

American kettle advertising sign in metal with iron handle, 22½in. high. $500

Morse's Distemper, enamel sign by Hassall, 60 x 40in. $695

Enameled sign for Fry's Chocolate by Chromo, Wolverhampton, 30 x 36in. $765

KITCHENWARE

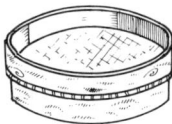

Victorian wooden
sieve. $10

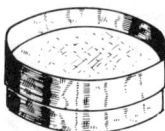

19th century brass
sieve. $65

An unusual 19th century
sieve enclosed in copper
oval container, complete
with carrying handles,
circa 1850. $170

SKEWERS

Silver skewer, 1902. $75

Silver meat skewer by Wallace and
Hayne, London 1819. $190

Meat skewer by Wallace and Hayne,
London, 1819. $215

Pair of silver meat skewers by Peter
and Ann Bateman, 1798. $225

SKIMMERS

Brass skimmer with pierced handle.
$35

Salamander, a hot metal plate for
browning food. $45

Cook's copper cream skimmer with
wrought iron handle, circa 1790.
$75

18th century brass skimmer
with iron handle. $160

SMOKING AIDS

Brass flake tobacco cutter, 3¼in. long, with small brass handle. $40

Lighter made to commemorate the Great War, in the shape of a brass and copper book, 2in. high. $30

A circular carved wood tobacco jar. $55

Solid brass pipe stopper, circa 1830, 1½in. high. $65

Early 20th century brass smoker's stand. $75

Pratts ethyl gasolene lighter fuel dispenser. $180

17th century Dutch copper and brass tobacco box, 6¼in. wide. $400

Silver table lighter on black marble base, by E. H. Stockwell, London, 1879, 15.5cm. long. $505

Early gas cigarette lighter, brass, probably English, circa 1880, 20in. high. $525

KITCHENWARE

SPICE BOXES

Small japanned spice box, black with gilt decoration. $35

Circular table spice box complete with nutmeg grater, circa 1830, 7in. diam. $135

Table square spice box with named section interior, circa 1840. $170

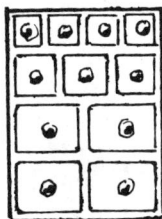

Pinewood spice drawers with brass pulls, circa 1820, 14½in. high x 11½in. x 7in. $200

Small oak spice cupboard with eight interior drawers, circa 1690. $450

Mid 17th century oak spice cabinet, 15in. wide. $675

One of three George III lignum vitae spice grinders each in three parts, with screw-on lids. $1,320

Oak spice box, 17th century. $1,745

Jewish parcel gilt spice box, mid 18th century, 11¼in. high, 9oz.5dwt. $3,825

SPINNING WHEELS

19th century beechwood spinning wheel. $110

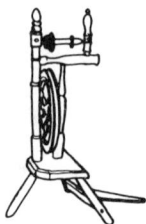

18th century oak spinning wheel. $200

19th century Continental pinewood spinning wheel. $200

Oak and elm spinning wheel. $275

18th century oak spinning wheel. $300

Rare twin spindle spinning wheel, 4ft.4in. high. $330

Early 19th century Flemish painted beech spinning wheel with treadle, 48in. high. $335

Antique fruitwood spinning wheel. $350

Stripped pinewood farmhouse spinning wheel, circa 1820, 20in. diam. $355

KITCHENWARE

SPINNING WHEELS

Late 18th century Dutch walnut and fruitwood spinning wheel. $400

18th century upright fruitwood spinning wheel, 31in. high. $450

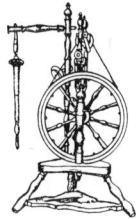

Fine quality beechwood spinning wheel. $635.

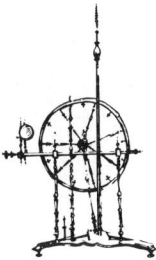

Superb early 19th century silk spinning wheel. $690

19th century beechwood spinning wheel on three bobbin-turned supports, 2ft.8in. high. $715

Walnut and beechwood spinning wheel, 18th century, with spindle spoke wheel and frame, 23in. wide. $1,150

Late 19th century satinwood spinning wheel with detachable top, 1.16m. high. $1,170

18th century fruitwood spinning wheel. $2,000

Rare late 18th century brass spinning wheel on mahogany stand, 35in. high. $3,510

SPITS

19th century brass roasting jack. $65

A rare polished steel Larkspit, 30½in. high, circa 1750. $160

Rare steel spitjack, circa 1700. $845

A superb example of a William and Mary period wrought iron meat spitjack, 12in. high, circa 1690. $955

Queen Anne mechanical iron spitjack, circa 1700, 13in. high. $1,075

George III brass and steel spitjack, stamped P. Pearson, 11in. high. $1,190

SPOON RACKS

Oak spoon rack in three layers, 30cm. wide. $135

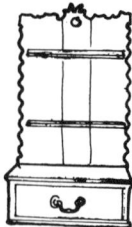

George I oak and walnut spoon rack, 26in. high. $585

18th century American decorated pine spoon rack, 12¾in. long. $850

188

KITCHENWARE

SPOONS

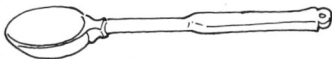

Large Victorian wooden spoon. $20

Early Scottish horn spoon. $30

Victorian silver berry spoon. $90

Early Georgian cast silver mote spoon. $125

STICKSTANDS

Victorian embossed brass oval stickstand. $65

An embossed brass and oak half circle stickstand, 2ft.7in. high. $90

Cast iron Gothic revival umbrella stand, about 1860, 30in. high.$1,000

STOCKPOTS

Victorian polished steel cooking pot. $35

Large copper stockpot with lid, circa 1820, 12in. diameter$180

A polished copper stockpot, complete with brass tap and copper carrying handles, circa 1820, 13in. diameter. $270

STOVES

French cast iron stove finished in mid brown vitreous enamel, circa 1920, 20in. square. $85

Belgian cast iron stove in dusty-pink vitreous enamel, circa 1925, 19in. high. $105

Late 19th century cast iron stove with steel fittings. $135

Victorian cast iron stove in working order. $150

French cast iron stove finished in blue-gray vitreous enamel, circa 1920, 22in. high. $190

Late·19th century French green enameled cast iron stove by Montherme Lavel-Diel. $205

Belgian cast iron bow-fronted stove in blue/gray vitreous enamel, circa 1905, 29in. high. $220

Salamandre cast iron stove finished in mid green vitreous enamel, circa 1900, 23½in. wide. $250

French Poel a Bois 'Le Selecte' woodburning cast iron stove, circa 1910, 22in. high. $390

An unusual French Empire peat burning fire. $540

Belgian cast iron stove 'Derby' finished in dark green enamel, circa 1910, 43in. high. $560

French Godin 392 cast iron stove, circa 1920, 45in. high. $570

Pure wood burning stove in cast iron, circa 1880. $595

Cast iron Scandinavian pot stove, marked Aadals Brug No. 77, circa 1890's, 72in. high. $610

Belgian 'Westminster' free-standing stove, circa 1920, 25½in. high. $765

French Siveria Niledo cast iron bow-fronted stove, circa 1910, 28in. high. $980

Belgian Languillier cast iron and ceramic cooking range, circa 1910. $1,100

French Soughland 491 cast iron stove in green vitreous enamel, circa 1900, 30in. high. $1,300

STRAINERS

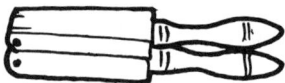

Wooden lemon squeezer with rounded place for half lemon. $15

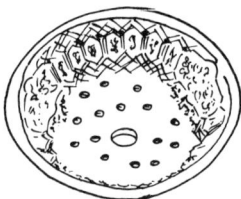

Victorian china water cress dish. $20

Early 20th century china tea strainer. $20

George I silver lemon strainer by Francis Knelme, London 1727. $450

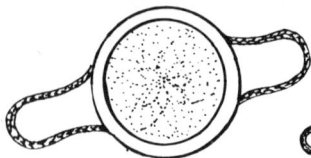

Silver lemon strainer by H. Northcote, 1799. $505

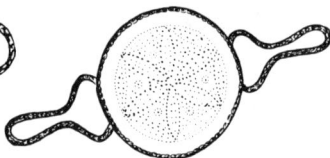

Unusual bright-cut silver strainer, 1778, 10in. across. $540

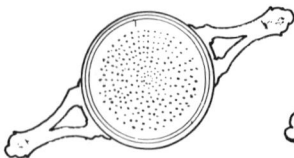

Large silver punch strainer by Robert Calderwood, Dublin, 1752, 11½in. long, 6oz. 5dwt. $1,350

Early 18th century silver lemon strainer by Thomas Bamford, 6in. long, 2oz. 4dwt. $1,520

192

KITCHENWARE

STRING HOLDERS

Victorian papier mache string holder. $30

Late 19th century transfer-printed string holder. $35

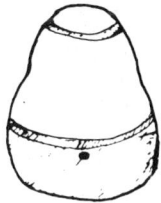

Yewwood string holder. $35

Yewwood string holder with ridged decoration. $45

Early 19th century lignum vitae string box, 5½in. high. $75

Model of a terrestrial globe in the form of a string box, 4¼in. high, circa 1890. $190

SUGAR CUTTERS

Steel sugar cutters, circa 1790. $45

18th century steel sugar cutters. $70

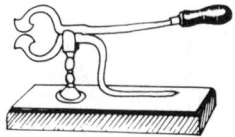

Pair of 18th century brass sugar cutters on a mahogany stand. $100

TANKARDS

19th century German carved
wood tankard surmounted
by a fox's head. $90

Early copper tankard with
brass rim. $130

19th century oak peg
tankard bound with two
bands of split twigs.
$220

Enameled milchglas tankard,
Spanish or Bohemian, circa
1780, 13.2cm. high.
$225

Scandinavian burrwood peg
tankard with carved lid,
8¼in. high. $435

Large engraved ale tan-
kard with bell bowl,
circa 1760, 20cm. high.
$720

Scandinavian wooden
tankard with inscribed
and dated silver plaque,
1743. $880

Early 19th century Norwe-
gian sycamore peg tankard,
22cm. high. $885

Meissen silver gilt mounted
tankard and cover, circa
1750. $1,630

Oak tantalus, inscribed Betjemanns Patent, with silver plated mounts and cut glass whisky decanters, 12in. high. $130

Three-bottle tantalus in brass bound case. $250

Small Victorian tantalus with three molded glass decanters. $250

Mid 19th century Black Forest tantalus of table cabinet form, 19in. high. $465

Oak decanter box, circa 1880, with Bramah lock, 13¾in. wide. $475

Victorian coromandel wood and brass tantalus with three bottles, 12in. wide. $620

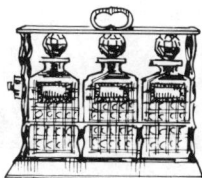

English silver-on-copper cut crystal decanter set by Betjemann's, 30cm. high. $700

Mid 19th century Continental amboyna wood and ebonized tantalus, interior fitted with four decanters and ten glasses. $790

Mid 19th century scarlet boulle tantalus with fitted interior, 13½in. wide. $1,080

195

TEA CADDIES

A birch oblong tea caddy, decorated with transfer printed view of Ford Castle. $70

Early 19th century covered oval quill work box with ivory finial, 5½in. long. $170

Mid 19th century amboyna wood oval shaped tea caddy, 14.5cm. wide. $205

Mid 19th century coromandel wood tea caddy, 38cm. wide.$270

Red tole painted tea caddy and writing box, circa 1790, 8in. wide. $300

Rare George III embroidered tea caddy of hexagonal shape, circa 1775, 7½in. wide. $305

Regency mother-of-pearl tea caddy of bow-fronted form, 8in. wide.
          $340

George III rolled paperwork tea caddy, circa 1785, 6¼in. wide, slightly chipped. $370

Regency mother-of-pearl and tortoiseshell tea caddy, 7in. wide, circa 1820. $595

KITCHENWARE

TEA CADDIES

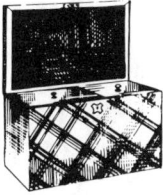

Tartan tea caddy by Chas. Stiven, Laurencekirk, circa 1830, 20cm. wide. $625

Rare Pontypool oval tea caddy painted in gilt and red, about 1780, 5½in. high. $720

One of a pair of tin tea storage bins by Henry Troemner, Philadelphia, circa 1870, 22½in. high. $750

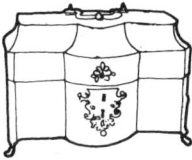

Rare early Georgian caddy case of wood covered with shagreen and mounted with silver, 7in. high. $1,000

Red Toleware tea caddy with two canisters, English, about 1790, 5¾in. high. $1,080

An interesting oak tea caddy made of timbers from HMS Victory. $1,090

Rare George II palisander wood tea caddy, 6¾in. high by 11in. wide. $1,125

Late 18th century tea caddy entirely veneered in mother-of-pearl with silver handles and ball and claw feet, 6½in. high. $1,800

Louis XVI marquetry tea caddy with molded corners, circa 1775, 22cm. wide. $2,125

197

TEA CADDIES
CHINA

Art Deco china tea caddy in the form of a Chinese man. $35

Pearlware tea caddy of canted rectangular form, 13cm. high, circa 1860. $225

Ludwigsburg oval tea caddy with metal cover, circa 1770, 13.5cm. high. $335

Meissen arched rectangular tea caddy and cover, circa 1740-50, 13cm. high. $445

Worcester Dr. Wall period tea caddy and cover decorated with flowers and insects, 4¾in. tall. $470

Meissen arched rectangular tea caddy and cover, stippled with cupids, circa 1755, 11cm. high. $520

A Lowestoft porcelain tea caddy, with chinoiserie decoration. $620

A Prattware tea caddy depicting George III, 6¼in. high, 1780-90. $675

Whieldon square tea caddy, circa 1760, 12.5cm. high. $675

CHINA

Ludwigsburg arched rectangular tea caddy with Ozier border, circa 1765, 12.5cm. high. $685

Early Frankenthal arched rectangular tea caddy and cover painted with large birds, circa 1756, 16cm. high. $830

Meissen arched rectangular tea caddy and cover, borders edged with gilt, circa 1765, 12cm. high. $1,015

Mid 19th century Japanese Satsuma earthenware caddy and cover, 13.5cm. high. $1,040

Rare Coalport 'jeweled' tea caddy on a pink ground, printed crown mark, 1890-1910, 6in. high. $1,070

Kangxi tea caddy of rectangular form, 4½in. high, on bracket feet. $1,070

Bristol delft tea caddy of octagonal form, circa 1760-70, 4¼in. high. $1,730

Meissen chinoiserie rectangular tea caddy painted by C. F. Herold. $1,850

Meissen tea caddy and cover, 10.5cm. high, circa 1725. $2,250

199

TEA CADDIES
FRUITWOOD

A Victorian fruitwood oblong sarcophagus shaped tea caddy, 11in. wide. $80

A fruitwood sarcophagus shaped tea caddy, circa 1820. $115

George III rectangular tea caddy banded in kingwood and boxwood, 23cm. wide. $135

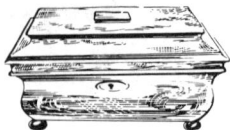

Unusual fruitwood tea caddy, circa 1830, 10½in. wide, with rosewood lidded tea containers. $195

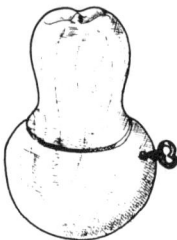

Georgian fruitwood tea caddy in the shape of a pear, and with its original lock and key.$450

George III fruitwood tea caddy, 10.5cm. high. $500

George III fruitwood tea caddy in the form of a gourd with stalk, circa 1800, 5½in. high. $525

An unusual pair of applewood tea caddies, circa 1780. $1,250

One of a pair of George III canteloup-shaped tea caddies, 4½in. wide. $2,250

KITCHENWARE

GLASS

TEA CADDIES

19th century ruby glass circular box and cover, 4in. diam. $90

Victorian slagware caddy, circa 1870, 5½in. high. $170

Rare Staffordshire 'enamel' tea bottle, 5½in. high, circa 1760. $675

Rare enameled armorial rectangular tea caddy and stopper, 7in. high. $2,025

One of a pair of glass tea caddies similar to enamel work carried out in Staffordshire. $6,000

One of a pair of Staffordshire opaque white glass tea caddies, 14.2cm. high. $7,315

HAREWOOD

George III harewood and satinwood marquetry tea caddy, circa 1770. $320

George III oval harewood tea caddy, 5½in. wide. $565

George III harewood and marquetry caddy with flower vignettes, about 1790, 5in. high. $675

TEA CADDIES
IVORY

George III ivory veneered tea caddy of oval shape, lid with pineapple finial, circa 1790. $350

Ivory tea caddy with rosewood stringing. $505

Late 18th century Russian walrus ivory casket, from the Kholmorgory region, 19.2cm. wide. $640

Gold mounted ivory veneered tea caddy. $705

George III ivory tea caddy, 4¼in. wide, circa 1790. $730

George III ivory veneered tea caddy of decagonal shape, 6¼in. long. $955

George III ivory and pewter tea caddy, 5in. high. $1,015

18th century Eastern carved ivory tea caddy with original glass bottles. $1,180

A good 18th century pierced ivory tea caddy. $1,720

LACQUERED

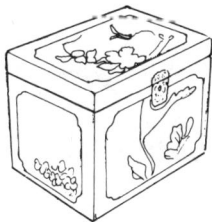

Japanese lacquered box decorated with flowers. $90

19th century Chinese lacquered tea caddy with fitted interior. $140

19th century octagonal, black and gilt lacquered two division caddy in the Chinese style. $170

Late 19th century Kashmir lacquered box. $180

A Chinese black lacquer octagonal tea caddy, decorated with figures, in gold, fitted with two pewter containers, 11in. wide. $200

A Chinese black, red and gold lacquer octagonal tea caddy, the interior fitted with two pewter containers, 14in. wide. $200

19th century lacquered box and cover, Japanese, 22cm. wide. $585

Unusual 19th century Chinese black lacquer tea caddy. $1,015

Rare George II japanned tea caddy, circa 1740, 10¼in. wide. $1,015

TEA CADDIES
MAHOGANY

Georgian mahogany tea
caddy with a brass handle
and boxwood inlay.
$80

Mahogany oblong tea caddy
with satinwood shell motifs.
$100

A Georgian mahogany
oblong ogee shaped tea
caddy with brass han-
dle. $115

Victorian mahogany and
brass bound tea caddy
inset with white stones.
$115

Sheraton mahogany tea
caddy, with satinwood
and ivory key escutcheon,
on bun feet, circa 1805,
12in. long, 6in. wide, 6½in.
high. $135

Banded mahogany and
ebony string inlay domed
top tea caddy with glass
liner. $135

Small early 19th century
inlaid mahogany tea caddy.
$135

Regency casket-shaped
mahogany tea caddy, on
brass ball feet, circa 1820.
$135

Sheraton tea caddy in
mahogany and partridge-
wood, 5in. high.
$135

MAHOGANY

TEA CADDIES

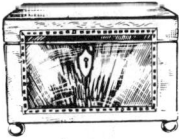

Sheraton period tea caddy, circa 1800, 7in. wide, in mahogany with ebony stringing. **$145**

Sheraton mahogany tea caddy, circa 1800, 12in. long. **$150**

Early Victorian mahogany tea caddy inlaid with mother-of-pearl decoration. **$160**

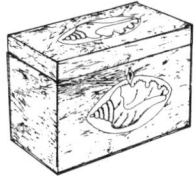

Sheraton tea caddy in mahogany and partridgewood, 6¼in. high. **$160**

Sheraton mahogany tea caddy, 19cm. wide. **$170**

George III mahogany tea caddy, front inlaid with satinwood conch shell motif, 7½in. wide, circa 1790. **$175**

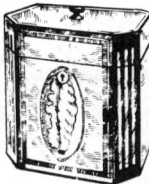

Chippendale period mahogany tea caddy, circa 1770, with brass handle, 11in. long. **$190**

Sheraton fiddle back mahogany tea caddy, 11.5cm. wide. **$225**

A Chippendale period mahogany tea caddy, containing three compartments and secret drawer. **$225**

TEA CADDIES
MAHOGANY

Late 18th century mahogany
tea caddy, 7½in. wide.
$225

Georgian mahogany tea
caddy on shaped feet.
$260

George III mahogany
and satinwood tea
caddy, circa 1780.
$300

Sheraton fiddle back
mahogany two divi-
sion tea caddy inlaid
with marquetry,
17.5cm. wide.
$340

George III mahogany and
kingwood three division tea
caddy, 31cm. wide.
$340

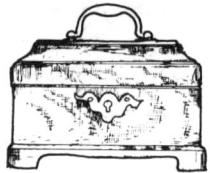

Early mahogany caddy
case with original tin
caddies inside, 4in.
high. $500

Sheraton mahogany caddy
inlaid with roses.
$340

Large Georgian crossban-
ded tea caddy with brass
handle, 14½in. wide.
$1,150

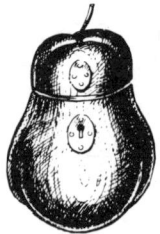

Mahogany and iron tea
caddy in the shape of a
pear. $1,215

PAPERWORK   **TEA CADDIES**

18th century octagonal
caddy of curled paper
design with leaf sprays.
$280

George III tea caddy ven-
eered in rolled paper, 18cm.
wide. $325

Sheraton period satinwood
inlaid octagonal tea caddy
with paperwork and glazed
panels, 17cm. wide.
$475

George III rolled paper-
work tea caddy, circa
1790. $430

George III rolled paper tea
caddy, 7¼in. high.
$675

George III rolled paper-
work tea caddy, 8¼in.
wide. $810

Late 18th century rolled
paperwork tea caddy,
inset with picture of girl.
$855

Late 18th century rolled
paperwork tea caddy,
inset with picture of a
girl. $1,095

Very rare late 18th century
rolled paper tea caddy,
English, 5in. high.
$1,350

TEA CADDIES
PAPIER MACHE

Double papier mache tea caddy, molded top inlaid with mother-of-pearl, 8¼in. wide. $125

Mid 19th century papier mache tea caddy of square form, 5in. square. $165

Papier mache box by Jennens & Bettridge, circa 1850, 11in. wide. $180

Russian hand painted papier mache tea caddy with maker's name in the foiled interior. $190

Mid Victorian rectangular painted and gilt papier mache tea caddy, 13in. wide. $205

Early 19th century papier mache tea caddy. $250

PENWORK

Regency penwork tea caddy, 9in. wide. $395

Fine Regency caddy of penwork illustrating 'The Fortune Teller', 5in. high. $720

An ivory and penwork tea casket, Vizagapatam, circa 1800. $945

PLATED   TEA CADDIES

Late 19th century
silver plated caddy.
$45

Silver plate Victorian
tea caddy, circa 1890,
6½in. high. $55

George III plated tea caddy.
$55

Victorian copper,
plated tea caddy,
7in. high. $90

Silver plated tea caddy.
$135

Sheffield plate caddy with
a solid silver plate engraved
with a crest set into the
front, 1800-10, 4½in. high.
$170

One of a pair of early 19th
century Sheffield plate tea
caddies. $170

Sheffield plate caddy,
about 1775-80, with typi-
cal Adam decoration and,
unusually, a lock.
$305

Oval Sheffield plate tea
caddy, 4½in. wide, with
bright cut engraving.
$520

TEA CADDIES ROSEWOOD

Regency rosewood tea caddy of casket form, 35cm. wide. $45

Small Victorian rosewood tea caddy, inlaid with mother-of-pearl. $80

Regency rosewood tea caddy, with mother-of-pearl inlaid lid, 35cm. wide. $85

Regency rosewood tea caddy with bombe front, 37cm. wide. $115

A Regency rosewood and sarcophagus-shaped tea caddy, the interior with two lidded compartments flanking the mixing bowl. $135

Early 19th century rosewood tea caddy inlaid with brass. $180

Rosewood two division tea caddy strung with boxwood decoration, 21cm. wide. $180

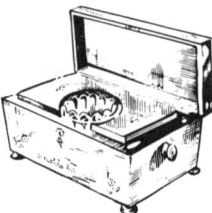

Regency rosewood tea caddy inlaid with mother-of-pearl, 12in. long. $305

Regency tea caddy, inlaid with brass and mother-of-pearl floral design. $370

KITCHENWARE

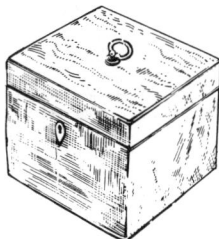

Victorian satinwood square-
shaped tea caddy, 11cm.
wide. $180

Georgian satinwood in-
laid tea caddy. $185

Victorian satinwood and
crossbanded square-sha-
ped tea caddy, 13.5cm.
wide. $190

A Sheraton satinwood and
inlaid tea caddy, circa 1790.
              $225

George III satinwood tea
caddy with marquetry in-
lay, about 1780, 5in. high.
              $260

Sheraton style tea caddy
of satinwood and rose-
wood, circa 1795.
          $280

George III rectangular
satinwood tea caddy, 6in.
wide. $350

George III inlaid satin-
wood caddy with silver
mounted glass containers.
              $500

George III oval satinwood
tea caddy with hinged lid,
6in. wide. $675

TEA CADDIES
SILVER

Late Victorian silver tea caddy, 11oz. **$170**

A Continental silver, square, tapering tea caddy and cover, 5½in. high, 7oz. **$170**

Guild of Handicrafts Ltd. silver tea caddy, London, 1906, 7cm. high, on four ball feet. **$220**

Walker & Hall Ltd., bombe tea caddy and cover, Sheffield, 1899, 14.5cm. high, 429gm. **$355**

Drum-shaped tea caddy and cover by Hunt & Roskell, London, 1856, 10.7cm. high, 13.7oz. **$610**

George III oval tea caddy and cover by H. Chawner, London, 1786, 12oz. **$765**

George II silver tea caddy, heavily embossed. **$825**

George I octagonal tea caddy by Sarah Holliday, 1725, 7oz. **$985**

George III oval-shaped silver tea caddy with beaded edges and urn finial, by Aug. Le Sage, London, 1779, 11½oz. **$1,090**

SILVER

TEA CADDIES

Silver tea canister by
Joseph Fainell, 1720.
$1,180

George III two division
tea caddy by Daniel
Pontifex, London, 1797,
19oz.13dwt., 7in. high.
$1,575

George III tea caddy, marked on base and cover, by
Robert Hennell, London,
1782, 4in. high, 13oz.2dwt.
$1,575

One of two George II
bombe tea caddies in
sizes, by Emick Romer,
London, 1762, 5¼in. high,
19oz.5dwt. $1,750

George III shaped oval
tea caddy by Aldridge &
Green, London, 1783,
4¾in. high, 12oz.13dwt.
$3,310

18th century Dutch silver
tea caddy, maker's mark
I.B., Amsterdam, 1726,
8oz.7dwt. $3,375

George III square tea caddy
engraved with imitation
Chinese characters, maker's
mark AL, 1786, 14oz.7dwt.
$3,375

George III drum-shaped
tea caddy by John Vere
and Wm. Lutwyche, Lon-
don, 1768, 4in. high, 15oz.
9dwt. $3,600

Silver tea caddy by Paul de
Lamerie, 1724, 13.3cm.
high, 15oz.13dwt.
$13,500

213

TEA CADDIES
TORTOISESHELL

Mid 19th century tortoiseshell two-division tea caddy with fluted front, 7½in. wide. $165

Serpentine fronted tortoiseshell tea caddy. $170

George III tortoiseshell tea caddy with silver mountings, 18cm. wide. $170

Regency tortoiseshell-veneered tea caddy with engraved plaque, circa 1820, 7¼in. wide. $175

Tortoiseshell two division tea caddy strung with pewter, 15.5cm. wide. $180

19th century tortoiseshell tea caddy inlaid with mother-of-pearl, 22cm. wide. $190

Tortoiseshell two division tea caddy strung with pewter and applied with mother-of-pearl, 20cm. wide. $190

Tortoiseshell two division tea caddy inlaid with mother-of-pearl, 8in. wide. $225

Tortoiseshell two division tea caddy with ivory feet, 18.5cm. wide. $250

KITCHENWARE

TORTOISESHELL

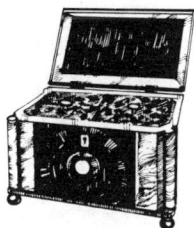

TEA CADDIES

Tortoiseshell two division tea caddy, 17.5cm. wide. **$280**

Regency tortoiseshell single compartment tea caddy with silver mounts, circa 1820, 5½in. high. **$290**

Regency tortoiseshell tea caddy with silver escutcheon and ivory mounted lid, circa 1820, 6¾in. wide. **$290**

Regency tortoiseshell two-division tea caddy with serpentine front, 7½in. wide, circa 1820. **$315**

19th century Tunbridge-ware tea caddy with floral inlay. **$315**

George IV tortoiseshell tea caddy, circa 1825, 7in. wide. **$350**

19th century tortoiseshell tea caddy. **$405**

Regency mother-of-pearl inlaid tortoiseshell veneered tea caddy, circa 1820, 6¾in. wide. **$430**

Early 19th century tortoiseshell tea caddy, inlaid with mother-of-pearl. **$450**

TEA CADDIES
TORTOISESHELL

Tortoiseshell tea caddy with engraved plate on front. $550

Tortoiseshell and silver tea caddy, 1896, 11cm. wide. $565

Late Victorian tortoiseshell and silver mounted tea caddy. $580

Tortoiseshell and motherof-pearl inlaid tea caddy. $720

Rare George III maplewood and tortoiseshell tea caddy, 6in. wide, circa 1780. $815

Late 18th century decagonal tea caddy of tortoiseshell with ivory banding and a silvered plaque, 5in. high. $855

Early 19th century silver mounted tortoiseshell casket with domed lid, 8¼in. wide. $1,550

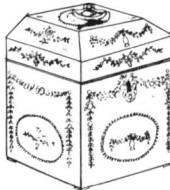

18th century tortoiseshell and silver pique tea caddy, silver mounted, 12.5cm. high. $1,880

Late 17th century Dutch East Indies tortoiseshell and silver mounted casket, 7¾in. long. $2,060

TUNBRIDGEWARE

TEA CADDIES

Tunbridgeware tea caddy.
$115

Victorian parquetry tea caddy with glass liner.
$160

Dome topped tea caddy in Tunbridgeware, 6in. wide. $180

19th century Tunbridgeware domed tea caddy.
$190

Large 19th century Tunbridgeware caddy.
$250

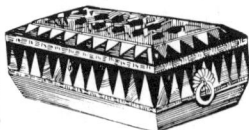

Regency Tunbridgeware box inlaid with cube pattern, circa 1820, 12in. wide. $305

Mid 19th century rosewood Tunbridgeware tea caddy by William Upton, inlaid with cube marquetry, 12½in. wide. $360

Regency Tunbridgeware tea caddy of octagonal shape, circa 1820, 6in. wide. $470

Tunbridgeware rosewood tea caddy with fitted interior, circa 1840, 13½in. wide. $665

TEA CADDIES
WALNUT

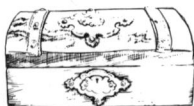

Late 19th century European walnut veneer tea caddy, brass and ivory-bound, 30cm. wide. $85

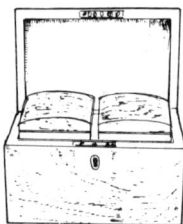

Walnut oblong tea caddy with domed cover. $90

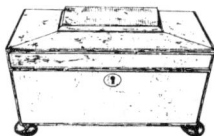

Victorian burr-walnut tea caddy on bun feet. $90

Fine quality 19th century walnut and brass mounted tea caddy with a glass liner. $170

Burr-walnut tea caddy, circa 1830, 15½in. wide. $190

Queen Anne tea caddy of veneered walnut on oak with chevron crossbanding on the lid and original handle and escutcheon, circa 1700, 9in. long. $395

YEWWOOD

Burr yew tree tea caddy, circa 1830. $100

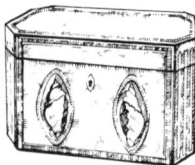

Sheraton yewwood two division tea caddy, 19cm. wide. $225

Yewwood two division tea caddy inlaid with mother-of-pearl, 22cm. wide. $225

KITCHENWARE

TEA CANISTERS

Victorian, Chinese style, tin tea caddy. $25

Two of six black japanned tea canisters, decorated with Chinese gilt design, 17in. high. $160

Part of a set of six green japanned tea canisters, 17in. high. $190

TEA URNS

One of a pair of Tole green chestnut vases and covers, 12in. high, circa 1800. $360

Large tea caddy in figured mahogany, 21in. high. $450

Sheraton period tea caddy in inlaid partridgewood, 9½in. high. $545

19th century Dutch marquetry octagonal tea chest, 13in. wide. $810

Mahogany urn-shaped caddy, circa 1790, 9in. high, with ivory finial. $970

Pair of Pontypool urns and covers, 13in. high. $1,035

TEAPOTS

Victorian red enamel
teapot. $15

Edwardian silver lustre
teapot and stand. $20

Spode's Imperial covered
teapot with gadrooned
and leaf moldings, circa
1810. $35

Liverpool teapot ename-
led in black and gilding,
Herculaneum factory,
circa 1805. $75

19th century Japanese
patinated brass teapot
of bulbous form with
wrapped handle grip,
.6in. diam. $80

Superb Rockingham
rococo-shaped porce-
lain teapot and cover,
circa 1830. $105

19th century Staffordshire
'barge' teapot, 13in. high.
                            $165

Kinkozan earthenware
teapot and cover, painted
and gilt, circa 1900,
12.5cm. high. $205

Electroplated teapot, designed
by Christopher Dresser, on
triangular stand with burner,
19.5cm. high. $215

Walker & Hall silver tea kettle, London, 1886, 13cm. high, 17oz. $270

Derby teapot decorated with a traditional Imari pattern. $270

A Samson globular octangular teapot and cover, 18cm. wide. $295

Mid 18th century Qianlong teapot decorated with coats-of-arms, 5½in. high. $320

Worcester Dr. Wall teapot. $400

Circular teapot by Edward Barnard & Sons, London, 1852, 18.1oz., 13cm. high. $400

Victorian teapot in 'aesthetic' movement taste, by Francis Elkington, 1880, 21oz. $470

A rare Coronation Day teapot and cover, transfer-printed in black with two portraits of Queen Victoria and Windsor Castle, 1838, 24.8cm. (cracked). $475

Kangxi blue and white beehive-shaped teapot and cover with rectangular arch handle, 6½in. high. $570

KITCHENWARE

TEAPOTS

Worcester teapot, circa
1758-60, 4in. high, in underglaze blue. $640

Whieldon oviform teapot
and cover with crabstock
spout and handle, circa
1755, 19cm. wide. $650

Pear-shaped teapot by
Tessiers Ltd., London,
1927, 30.1oz. $660

Staffordshire saltglaze polychrome Jacobite teapot
and cover, circa 1745,
12.5cm. high. $700

Worcester teapot and
cover depicting 'The
Beckoning Chinaman',
circa 1755, 6¼in. high.
$800

George III oval teapot by
William Plummer, Lon-
don, 1787, 16oz.11dwt.,
5in. high. $830

Wedgwood & Bentley
teapot and cover in
black basalt, 13cm. high.
$860

Ludwigsburg porcelain teapot, spherical shape tapering to base, circa 1775,
4¾in. high. $875

George III silver teapot
and stand by Duncan
Urquhart and Naphtali
Hart, 19½oz. $900

KITCHENWARE

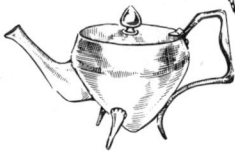

Electroplated teapot and cover designed by Christopher Dresser, 1880, 18cm. wide. $925

Henry Wilkinson & Co. compressed melon-shaped silver teapot, Sheffield, 1842, 827gm. $925

Rare Plymouth teapot and cover, 6½in. high, about 1768-70. $1,015

A very rare Meissen 'Japonnaise' teapot and cover, circa 1875. $1,170

Unusual Royal Worcester pierced and double-walled teapot and cover, dated for 1881, 7in. high. $1,260

An attractive Chelsea petal mounted teapot and cover, 6in. high, 1752-56. $1,350

Silver teapot and stand by Peter and Ann Bateman, 18½oz.$1,800

Staffordshire saltglaze teapot and cover, 7½in. wide. $2,025

Rare Ludwigsburg teapot and cover supported on three twig feet, 13cm. high, circa 1770. $3,870

KITCHENWARE

TEASETS

Late 19th century Limoges porcelain tea service with gilt floral details. $200

Part of a Clarice Cliff 'bizarre' tea service, twenty-four pieces, 1930's. $270

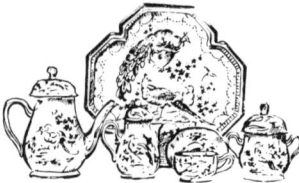

Late 19th century Samson tete-a-tete, tray 26.5cm. wide. $325

Part of a Davenport tea and coffee service, circa 1870, sixty-one pieces. $350

Good Minton solitaire set, date code for 1862. $380

Liberty & Co. 'Tudric' pewter tea service by Archibald Knox. $400

Part of a late 19th century Naples coffee set of seventeen pieces, pot 20.3cm. high. $435

A Limoges porcelain coffee service, designed by Jean Luce, 1920's. $475

'Bizarre' painted glazed pottery breakfast set, 1930's. $495

Newport pottery 'bizarre' one-person breakfast set, designed by Clarice Cliff, 1930's. $500

Coalport Felspar porcelain part tea and coffee service. $530

Newport pottery 'bizarre' two-person breakfast set, designed by Clarice Cliff, 1930's. $535

Part of a Copeland tea and coffee service of eighty-two pieces, circa 1900. $565

Hannah Barlow teaset, dated 1881, each piece incised with a frieze of rabbits. $695

Part of a good John Ridgway tea service, each piece painted with flowers, circa 1840. $715

Berlin part teaset, mid 19th century, each piece gilt decorated. $790

TEASETS

Small Charles Stuart Harris three-piece silver teaset, London, 1878, 77gm.
$835

Part of an eleven-piece Moorcroft coffee service in 'Hazledene' pattern. $945

Three-piece teaset with vase-shaped bodies, by Martin, Hall & Co. Ltd., London, 1879, 48.4oz. $990

Late 19th century Indian silver teaset, of four pieces, 3,778gm. $1,060

Part of a Flight, Barr & Barr period Worcester tea and coffee service. $1,225

Newport pottery 'Fantasque' two-person breakfast set, designed by Clarice Cliff, 1930's. $1,280

Swansea cabaret, painted with garden flowers, circa 1817. $1,440

Victorian tea and coffee service by J. Round & Son, Sheffield, 1884. $1,520

Part of a Spode part tea and coffee service painted in Imari style, circa 1820. $1,560

Part of a twenty-six-piece **Barr Worcester** tea and coffee service, circa 1792-1804. $1,770

Part of a Copeland part tea and coffee service of thirty-one pieces, circa 1825. $1,895

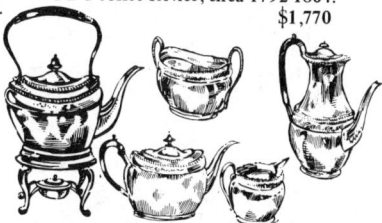

Edward VII engraved tea and coffee service, Sheffield, 1901-03, 86oz. $2,295

Swansea cabaret set complete with matching tray, 1814-17. $2,700

Late Meissen tete-a-tete of twelve pieces, crossed swords in blue. $2,590

Early 19th century Dutch four-piece teaset, 57oz.15dwt. $2,925

William Hutton & Sons Ltd. silver Art Nouveau tea and coffee service with tray, London, 1902-07. $3,825

TINS

Miniature tin of Andrews
Liver Salts produced by
LNER trains, circa 1930.
$10

Caleys Jazz-time toffee tin,
circa 1920. $20

1930's 'Players Navy Cut'
tobacco tin, 10 x 7.5cm.
$20

A large confectionery tin
by John Buchanan, Glas-
gow, 8¾in. wide, circa
1890. $25

Rowntree's toffee tin,
circa 1930. $25

Decorated mustard tin
showing National Games.
$55

One of a pair of 'Victory
V' urn tins in pre-
Raphaelite style, 1ft.0½in.
high. $70

Victory 'cradle' tin, English,
circa 1890. $480

Rectangular gilt metal
mosaic box, circa 1820,
3¾in. wide. $600

TOAST RACKS

19th century plated toast rack. $35

Toast rack by Walker & Hall, 1899, 7oz. $115

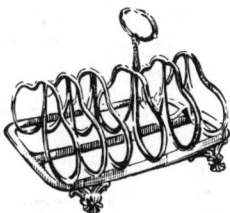

Early Victorian six-section toast rack by Henry Wilkinson & Co., 1839, 8oz. $190

Victorian toast rack by Robert Garrard, London 1869. $280

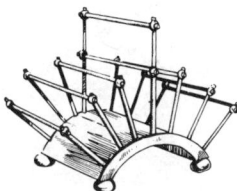

Hukin & Heath electroplated toast rack designed by Christopher Dresser, 1881, 12.5cm. high. $360

One of a pair of lyre-shaped toast racks by A., F. & A., Pairpoint, London, 1929, 15.1oz., 20.5cm. high. $420

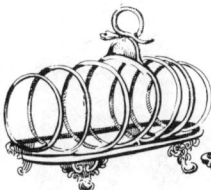

One of a pair of seven-bar toasters by Samuel Whitford, London, 1874, 17.7cm. long, 17.6oz. $870

Rockingham crested toast rack with three pierced gilt racks, circa 1835, 21cm. wide. $890

Large Elkington, Mason & Co. seven-bar silver toast rack, Birmingham, 1859, 759gm. $1,120

TOASTING FORKS

An early sycamore and walnut, steel toasting fork.　　$90

17th century brass and iron trivet toaster, 25in. long.　　$110

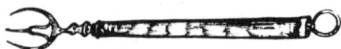

Silver toasting fork by Joseph Willmore, 1806.　　$260

George III Scottish bannock toaster, 27½in. long overall, Edinburgh, 1819.$640

TOBACCO CONTAINERS

Late 19th century English terracotta tobacco jar, 5in. tall.　　$55

18th century lead tobacco jar of octagonal shape with scroll decorative bands around the top and bottom rims of the base, 5¼in. high, 5in. long.　　$100

19th century Dutch brass tobacco box, lid etched with two figures in a landscape, 15cm. long.　　$170

Liberty pewter and enamel tobacco box with sides cast with rows of stylized leaves and set with blue-green enamel cabochons, 4¾in.　　$275

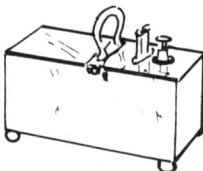

18th century brass coin-opening tobacco box, 9½in. long.　　$395

One of a set of six English mid 19th century tobacco containers, 1ft.5in. high. $2,080

KITCHENWARE

TONGS

Edwardian sugar tongs, Sheffield, 1908, ¾oz. $45

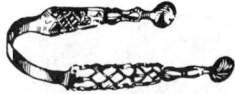

Pierced silver sugar tongs by William Tant, 1764. $80

Russian silver gilt and colored enamel tongs, circa 1900. $360

Early 18th century silver sugar tongs by L.E., London, circa 1710. $730

TOWEL RAILS

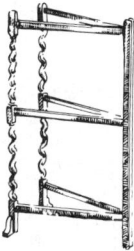

Edwardian oak towel rail with spiral supports. $45

Victorian mahogany triple towel rail. $65

Victorian mahogany framed towel rail. $80

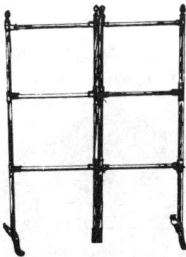

A late 18th century mahogany towel airer of two folding leaves, with boxwood stringing. $80

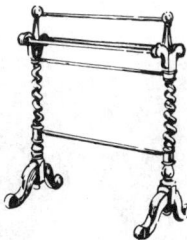

Victorian mahogany towel rail on twist supports. $90

Hepplewhite design towel horse, 2ft. $145

231

TRAYS

Large Indian brass tray, 2ft. wide.
$45

A Victorian oak tray with carved vine border and brass handles, 2ft. wide. $45

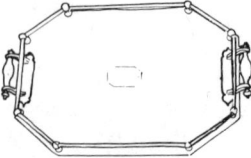

Edwardian oak double handled octagonal tea tray. $65

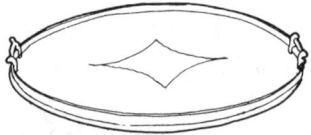

Mahogany inlaid oval tea tray with brass handles, 26½in. $65

Late 19th century butler's oak tray and folding stand. $65

Benares damascened circular coffee tray on a folding stand, 23in. diam. $65

An Indian brass oblong double handled tea tray, 19in. wide. $65

George III mahogany tray inlaid with a conch shell. $70

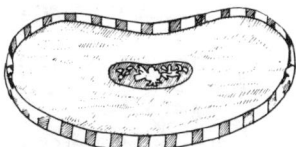

Edwardian mahogany kidney-shaped tray with marquetry center, 23in. wide. $90

A walnut and parquetry inlaid oblong tray with chess board and brass handles, 20½in. wide. $95

Early 20th century Edwardian mahogany tray with boxwood and mahogany gallery, 24in. wide. $140

Early 19th century toleware tray, probably Connecticut, 12½in. long. $150

Early 19th century black papier mache tray, 20¾in. long, with four shades of gilding. $170

Butchers' boy's shoulder meat carrier, circa 1810. $175

American decorated Tole tea tray with rolled rim, circa 1850, 26in. wide. $300

Edwardian mahogany tray and stand with painted decoration. $300

TRAYS

George III mahogany and brass bound tray, 23½in. long. $350

'Pontypool' tray with Napoleonic battle scene, circa 1820, 30in. x 21in. $370

Tole bread tray, probably New York, early 19th century, 13in. long. $370

A metal tray with pierced gallery decorated with an urn, flowers and birds, 2ft.3in. wide. $395

English black and gold papier mache tray, signed Jennens and Bettridge, approximately 30 x 22in., circa 1830. $480

Rare George I small walnut tray, 1ft.4¾in. wide. $500

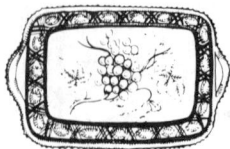

20th century Tuthill glass tray, signed, 13½in. long. $525

Georgian mahogany butler's tray complete with stand. $605

Emile Galle marquetry octagonal tray
inlaid with a landscape, 49.3cm. wide.
$885

Charles X ormolu and tole-peinte
tray, 23in. diam. $1,250

18th century red lacquer tray,
12¾in. long. $1,500

17th century early Lac Burgaute
tray, 13in. diam. $1,500

Gilt metal mounted oval Roman
mosaic tray, circa 1870, 40.5cm.
long. $1,510

Unusual Galle carved and inlaid
fruitwood tray, circa 1900.
$1,630

A square Japanese lacquer
chamfered tray, 16½in. wide.
$1,750

Early 18th century Florentine
Pietra Dura and ebony tray.
$14,000

TRIVETS

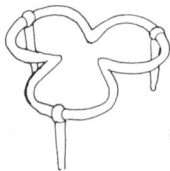

19th century Irish,
iron horse shoe trivet.
$35

Victorian brass trivet
with a turned wood
handle. $35

Victorian brass trivet
with screw-on legs.
$45

Victorian brass trivet.
$45

Late 18th century
brass trivet with
ebony handle. $65

Georgian brass trivet.
$85

Early 19th century trivet
with wooden handle.
$90

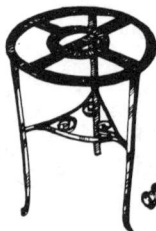

A heavy polished
steel Queen Anne
trivet, circa 1710,
13in. high, 10in.
diameter. $110

Early 19th century brass
lyre-shaped trivet with
wooden handle.$100

KITCHENWARE

TRIVETS

Interesting Victorian combined trivet and companion set. $115

Wrought iron trivet, circa 1740. $135

Fireside trivet in wrought iron with heavy pierced brass top and turned fruitwood handle, circa 1750. $135

TUBS

Wooden flour bin made by a cooper. $25

19th century brass bound tub. $135

One of a pair of brass bound tubs, circa 1850. $350

TUMBLERS

Victorian cranberry glass tumbler. $25

Victorian purple slag glass tumbler. $35

Engraved glass tumbler, 4¾in. high, circa 1790. $485

TUREENS

Doulton tureen with floral decoration, circa 1900. $45

Royal Worcester tureen decorated in gold, circa 1889. $55

'Gothic Castle' vegetable tureen, marked Spode. $90

Minton tureen with domed cover, circa 1868. $110

Blue printed Spode tureen, circa 1830. $170

Mason's ironstone tureen, circa 1830. $235

Minton game tureen, circa 1873. $235

Part of a Ridgway dessert service, circa 1825, nineteen pieces. $250

Early 19th century Meissen tureen, 43cm. wide. $305

Staffordshire saltglaze lobed oval two-handled tureen and cover, 27cm. wide, circa 1760. $495

18th century Chinese hexagonal tureen and cover, 23cm. high. $580

Mid 18th century European tin-glazed tureen and cover in the form of a bunch of asparagus, 16.5cm. wide. $680

Worcester blue and white tureen and cover, circa 1758. $935

One of a pair of 18th century clobbered blue and white tureens, covers and stands, 33cm. wide. $965

One of a pair of Derby oval sauce tureens and covers, circa 1813, 7.5cm. wide. $1,015

Faenza tureen and cover, circa 1760, 29cm. wide, sold with another. $1,610

One of a pair of Berlin royal presentation armorial quatre-foil sauce tureens and covers, circa 1775, 16.5cm. wide. $4,070

A rare pair of Chelsea partridge tureens and covers. $6,300

URNS

Victorian copper urn
with brass top. $75

A copper circular vase
shaped tea urn with
brass handles and spout,
13½in. high. $115

A George III brass
globular tea urn,
on four legs and
ball feet. £170

Doulton Lambeth urn
with raised stag and
foliage decoration,
16in. high. $190

Decorative large
copper and brass
George III tea urn,
22in. high. $215

Early 19th century
copper urn. $260

A gigantic toleware,
copper and brass tea
urn, originally used
as a grocer's shop
sign, circa 1850. $280

An 18th century copper
urn with brass tap.$305

A fine Sheffield vase
shaped tea urn with
scrolled handles and
chased and gadrooned
borders. $540

KITCHENWARE

VACUUM CLEANERS

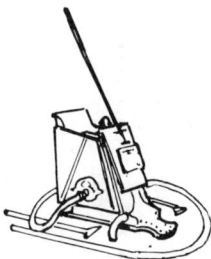

A 'Baby Daisy' vacuum cleaner. £35

Hand operated B.V.C. vacuum clearner, circa 1910. $215

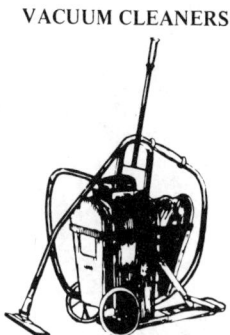

An early English vacuum-cleaner, with iron-spoked wheels and rubber tyres, 3ft.10in. high, circa 1900. $280

VEGETABLE CHOPPERS

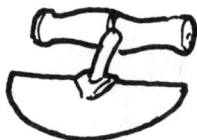

Mincing knife or suet chopper for use on a board. $15

Mincing knife or suet chopper for use on a board and with a bowl. $15

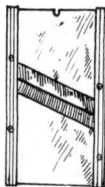

19th century wooden cabbage slicer. $55

Swedish steel vegetable chopper. $80

Large, Victorian kraut cutter of wood and brass. $80

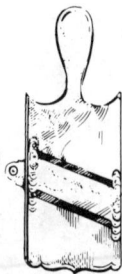

Early 19th century Dutch cucumber slicer, mounted on boxwood. $450

241

WARMING PANS

A 19th century brass bed warming pan, with long wood handle. $125

19th century copper warming pan. $145

Early 18th century brass warming pan with pierced front and flattened steel handle. $160

George III copper bed warming pan, circa 1760, 39in. long. $190

18th century copper warming pan with a turned fruitwood handle. $215

Dutch brass warming pan with pierced lid, dated 1619. 44in. long. $220

Early 17th century brass warming pan, pierced and punched, on steel handle. $505

James I brass warming pan with steel handle, dated 1620. $865

17th century English brass warming pan, pierced and decorated with a star motif. $1,245

KITCHENWARE

WASH BOILERS

Solid copper wash boiler, with turned over rim, circa 1830, 17in. diam., 13in. high. $110

Late 19th century copper wash boiler. $125

A large, solid copper wash boiler, the side seam and band near base with large copper rivets, circa 1820, 14in. high, 20in. diam. $125

WASHING EQUIPMENT

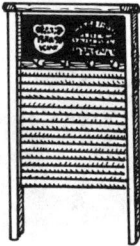

Late 19th century glass and wood scrubbing board. $10

A wooden sock stretcher, one of a pair. $20

Pine and elm dolly for washing clothes. $30

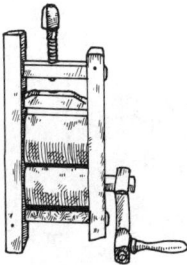

Scottish miniature wooden mangle for clerical bands. $55

Late 19th century mangle. $90

Late 19th century wood and iron rotary washer. $110

WATERING CANS

19th century English brass watering can.
$45

19th century brass watering can. $45

A Victorian brass water can, 11 in. high. $45

Victorian copper watering can. $55

A copper gallon water can with a swing handle and a brass loop handle.
$65

An oval lidded copper watering can, the body with molded banding.
$70

WEIGHTS

Cast brass bell-shaped butcher's scale weights, circa 1850, graduated sizes from 7lb-½oz., nine in all.
$235

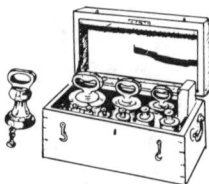

Set of thirty Halifax decimal bell metal weights in fitted mahogany case.
$2,380

Part of a set of ten brass weights, graduating from 100gm. to 20kg.
$3,025

A mahogany oblong box with brass handle on lid, 12in. long. $55

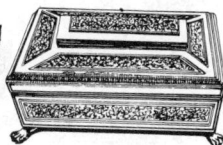

A Cairo carved wood and ivory workbox, with fitted interior, 13in. wide. $55

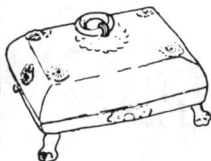

Victorian leather bound workbox with brass mounts and paw feet. $80

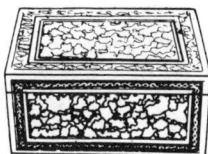

Chinese black lacquered box, 15in. wide. $80

Sarcophagus-shaped black and gold lacquer box with a scene of Chinese figures in a landscape. $90

Victorian burr-walnut and parquetry sewing box. $90

Tunbridgeware sewing box. $100

Lady's satinwood workbox, with ebony stringing and oval key escutcheon, circa 1795. $135

A Victorian rosewood inlaid and marquetry oblong workbox, 13in. wide. $170

WORKBOXES

A late 18th century chinoiserie lacquer box, circa 1790. $170

Japanese black lacquered octagonal workbox with hinged cover, 15½in. wide. $170

A Chinese black and gold lacquered octagonal box, the interior fitted with a tray with open and lidded compartments, 14in. wide. $180

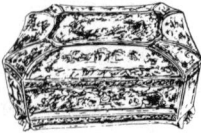

A Regency black lacquer sewing casket with slightly domed lid and canted corners, decorated with gilt chinoiseries. $210

Napoleonic prisoner of war straw workbox. $225

Mid 19th century rosewood Tunbridgeware casket with domed top, 10½in. wide. $245

Mid 19th century Anglo-Indian ivory workbox, 10½in. wide. $250

Tunbridgeware rosewood box, top inlaid with a view of Penshurst Place, circa 1870, 9in. wide. $270

Mid 19th century American painted wooden folk art box with hinged cover, 12in. long. $275

WORKBOXES

Rosewood Tunbridgeware box with floral mosaic lid and fitted interior, circa 1870, 9½in. wide. $305

Victorian papier mache sewing box. $310

Mid 19th century Tunbridgeware ash box with floral mosaic borders, 9½in. wide. $325

Mid 19th century papier mache sewing casket, fitted with lift-out tray, 13in. wide. $325

Black papier mache needlework box, circa 1840, 14in. long. $350

Mid 19th century Tunbridgeware rosewood pen box by William Upton, 9¾in. long. $360

Early 19th century strawwork casket with parquetry and floral marquetry borders, 12½in. wide. $385

Mid 19th century ivory Anglo-Indian workbox with gadrooned top and sides, 13½in. wide. $410

Tunbridgeware coromandel box by Thos. Barton, circa 1870, 9½in. wide. $450

WORKBOXES

19th century 'antler' sewing box with ivory compartments, 14in. wide. $550

Lacquered workbox with lift-up lid and four drawers. $565

Anglo-Indian ivory veneered workbox with gadrooned domed lid, 11¾in. wide. $675

19th century Goanese ivory and silver sewing box. $720

Tunbridgeware rosewood workbox with inlaid top and mosaic border, circa 1840, 10½in. wide. $740

George III woodworker's tool chest in a pine case, 3ft.6in. wide. $1,610

Coachbuilder's tool chest and contents, tools bearing the stamp of John Hartley, circa 1839. $3,200

Finely carved Oriental needlework box, fitted with compartments and ivory tools. $3,580

Rare Charles II needlework and micre casket, circa 1660. $3,600

INDEX

KITCHENWARE

KITCHENWARE

KITCHENWARE

KITCHENWARE

"The world's foremost reference book on antiques."
— *The New York Times*

THE
LYLE
OFFICIAL
ANTIQUES
REVIEW · 1983

*The Identification and Value Guide
with more than 10,000 illustrations*

At last, an antiques price guide—updated and published annually—that can make you rich! Share the privileged information of international dealers and collectors in the priceless pages of *The Lyle Official Antiques Review* which insiders have depended on for more than a decade.

More than 600 pages cover furniture, silver, glassware, ornaments, clocks, toys, gold, bric-a-brac and much, much more,—with every item precisely illustrated. Not only are the big-money auction buys here, but also the surprises you're likely to find in flea markets and antiques shops, in family garages and attics. Prices are based on actual sales records from over 150 auction houses and retail outlets in the United States and Europe. Wise buyers don't speculate about price and quality—they count on Lyle's 100 percent reliability. Follow their lead and mine the resources of *The Lyle Official Antiques Review.* It may well be the most valuable piece you'll ever invest in. *Index. Hardcover edition: $24.95. Flexible binding with jacket: $14.95.*

At your bookstore or order from Department LAV, Coward-McCann, Inc., 200 Madison Avenue, New York, NY 10016. Please add $1.60 for postage and handling to each order and state and local taxes where they apply. A complete list of all Lyle publications on antiques and of other books for collectors of antiques is available from Coward-McCann, Inc. upon request.

POCKET-SIZE IDENTIFICATION AND
PRICE GUIDES TO TWELVE CATEGORIES
OF POPULAR COLLECTIBLES

THE
LYLE
ANTIQUES
& THEIR VALUES

GLASS • FURNITURE
SILVER • CHINA
DOLLS & TOYS • ORIENTAL ANTIQUES
ART DECO/NOUVEAU • METALWORK
KITCHENWARE
MILITARIA • AMERICANA
CLOCKS

*Each book contains over
2,000 black-and-white illustrations.*

Compiled and designed by the staff of *The Lyle Official Antiques Review,* each of these handy volumes includes up-to-the minute prices for over 2,000 items. With detailed illustrations and precise descriptions, they provide dealers, collectors, and buyers with basic information on a broadly representative selection of specialized antiques. Pocket-size and bound in a flexible cloth binding, perfect for use in shops, flea markets, and at auctions, *The Lyle Antiques and Their Values* are your keys to smart antique buying. $5.95 each.

At your bookstore or order from Department LAV, Coward-McCann, Inc., 200 Madison Avenue, New York, NY 10016. Please add $1.60 for postage and handling to each order and state and local taxes where they apply. A complete list of all Lyle publications on antiques and of other books for collectors of antiques is available from Coward-McCann, Inc. upon request.